Cape Cod
Lucky

In Another Time

Dana Eldridge

Foreword by Greg O'Brien

Cover illustration by Douglas W. Turner of Turner Galleries, Chatham
Other illustrations by Louise Russell

Stony Brook Group
Brewster, Ma.

Published by Stony Brook Publishing & Productions, Inc.
25 Stony Hill Road
Brewster, Ma. 02631
(508-896-2514)

For ordering information contact the author at:
P.O. Box 576
East Orleans, MA 02643

ISBN: 1-887086-01-3

Cover design and page layout by Joe Gallante
Stony Brook Group

To all the grandchildren,
Eldridge and otherwise, so they might 'see' and 'know'
a Cape Cod of another time.

Acknowledgements

As always, this has not been a singular achievement. Help and suggestions came from all sides. Most heartwarming has been the favorable response for my first effort, *Once Upon Cape Cod*, which was a source of inspiration and the stimulus for this sequel.

Mostly we make our own 'luck', on rare occasions good fortune comes unbidden into our lives and we wonder how and why.

Thank you, Lynne, from a very lucky Cape Codder.

What others have said about Dana Eldridge's first book: *Once Upon Cape Cod*

"Dana Eldridge writes with an infectious sense of humor and an unembarrassed love of the past. This is a book of essays where time stands still, the way it should. His boyhood adventures remind you of Huckleberry Finn and Tom Sawyer. He had loving, laconic parents, and perfect grandparents. The whole watery world of Cape Cod was full of freedom and adventure for a boy. Here is the classic theme of local, small town life before we began to run away from it. It was an ideal many still look for, but seldom find. Yet these essays in Dana's parochial style gently pull us back. Cape Cod has not deserted its own proportions, in a run of fish, a clam flat, and the endlessly changing shores. We have only to stop, and go out looking for them."

—JOHN HAY, author of several books on nature, including *The Run* and *A Beginner's Faith In Things Unseen*.

"*Once Upon Cape Cod—from Cockle Cove to the Powder Hole* is absolutely delightful. It is important for all of us to know the Cape, and something about the people who lived here long before we came."

—JULIE HARRIS, actress

"Dana Eldridge, who gives us this glimpse into his love life is more than a good writer. He is, to our lasting benefit, a storyteller.

In the telling, he gives us—in almost a stream of consciousness style—wonderful essays about the early days of Chatham where he grew up, and even something of the Chatham that is there now and astonishingly little changed.

The luxury to which he was born was a cornucopia that debouched all the oysters one could eat, all the little necks one could want, all the snapper blues one could consume, and all the salty out-of-doors one could inhale.

A writer would have polished the material. Dana simply tells it, and it lives."

—JOHN A. ULLMAN, author, newspaper columnist.

Contents

Foreword

By Greg O'Brien

"We make our own luck," writes Dana Eldridge.

A 13th generation Cape Codder, Eldridge's good fortune is rooted in the 1600s when his ancestor, a cantankerous English weaver named William Nickerson, left Yarmouth because it was too crowded.

"He hitched up his ox team, gathered up his family and headed east to the largely unexplored lands of Cape Cod," Eldridge notes. "His internal compass must have been fixated on east because he stopped only when he could no longer go in that direction, settling in a land called by its few Native American inhabitants, Monomoyick. He liked the lay of this land… and wanted to possess it."

So he purchased from a local sachem, called the Old Sagamore, the northeast portion of what is now Chatham. And the rest, as they say, is history—family history.

Cape Cod Lucky–In Another Time, Eldridge's eloquent sequel to *Once Upon Cape Cod*, is a story of growing up on the Cape in the mid 40s and 1950s—one of the "last remnants of the unhurried life of the nineteenth century."

Eldridge's poignant narrative offers a reassuring anchor—a peaceful point of reference—as we look ahead to the changes, some of them life wrenching, and the challenges of a new millennium.

"You can't go home!" society declares. But Eldridge does, and in *Cape Cod Lucky* he brings all of us wash ashores along in the soothing wake of his charm.

"Cape Codders have a deserved reputation for not 'letting on,'" writes Eldridge. "They will take considerable pains to carefully conceal any feelings that may intrude in their lives... Good feelings, terrible feelings, it doesn't matter. Cape Codders don't want to let on, and they rarely do."

In *Cape Cod Lucky*, Eldridge opens that rare, isolated window to old Cape Cod so we can all breathe in the sweet, salty aroma of a simpler time. There is something about a Cape Cod summer or early fall that no other place, regardless of how peaceful and pastoral, can equal. The sky is simply brighter here, the sun more radiant, the air more pure.

We all seek some tangible connection to this land. Eldridge makes that connection for us to a Cape Cod we can only imagine, with his tales of people and places like: Shark Hole and wave-tossed Point Rip; blue crabbing as a small boy on pure tidal creeks; a twenty dollar Model A, the perfect car for the beach; Eldridge's close friend Warren Baker, one of the last true Cape Codders; and an 83-year-old grandmother who lived alone in an isolated island cottage accompanied only by a wood stove and hand pump for water.

"You'll smell the salt wind, you'll hear the surf roar, you'll hear the surf roaring on the bar, and you'll laugh out loud at the wonderfully wry stories that fill this book," promises William Martin, author of the best selling *Cape Cod*.

"Dana writes with an infectious sense of humor and an unembarrassed love of the past," says naturalist and author John Hay.

"Today, men and women, and even children, come by their hundreds of thousands and their traffic punishing miles to experience for a week or two what Dana Eldridge had when he stepped out the door," adds editor and author John Ullman.

"Ain't we lucky living on Cape Cod," Eldridge's good friend Baker observes at the end of this book.

And ain't we lucky to read all about it.

Greg O'Brien is editor and publisher of Stony Brook Publishing & Productions -- The Stony Brook Group -- and is editor of Cape Cod Life *magazine.*

Introduction

The Cape Cod in this book was, to me, just yesterday. It was a time when going barefoot in summer was the norm; wearing shoes was the surest way to be branded an outsider. Woods and fields were far more common than people. Fences were commonplace, and had a purpose: they were used to hold livestock in or keep them out. Outhouses were still in use, not often, but here and there around our small town.

Food gathering from the flats, from the sea, and from the marshes was as natural as breathing—everyone knew what quahogs were and where to find them. Every street had homes that had been sitting empty for decades. New construction was rare, real estate agents and land development did not exist. Indeed, land ownership was often a burden. The thought of advertising land for sale would be akin to advertising air for sale (although, now that I think of it, that isn't such a good analogy—just over the bridge in Wareham, some entrepreneur did a brisk business selling bottles of genuine Cape Cod air).

Change was all around us. When an airplane flew over, we all stopped what we were doing and craned our necks for a better look. Trains, once commonplace and economical transportation, were succumbing to the advancing ribbons of asphalt lacing the nation and the Cape. Coal and wood were being phased out in favor of oil as a means of heating the home, but the only real outside influence seemed to be the wondrous sound of the table radio.

When I was a boy, Cape Cod and the rest of the country had endured twelve years of a withering worldwide Depression and four years of a decimating world war. The Great Depression had little effect on my life and little effect on anyone I knew. It changed bank balances, but no one I knew went hungry, no one was put out in the cold, although the Packards, Hudsons and those sixteen-cylinder La Salles around town were often replaced by less-expensive Fords.

The world war was another story, and when it came looming over our horizon, it was impossible to ignore. It touched all of the families in town either directly or indirectly. But to the astonishment of many and the delight of all, the nation and the Cape rallied beyond all predictions and beyond all belief. Our world was saved and we, America, had saved it. We would all have plenty to feel good about for a long time to come. And little in our small Cape Cod world would ever be the same again.

Cape Cod Lucky—In Another Time begins in 1945, when I was four-teen-years-old, and is a sequel to my previous book, *Once Upon Cape Cod*. My goal in writing these books is that my children, my grandchildren, and all of us who love this slender peninsula, will see the essence of a Cape Cod in another time, a time that was not so very long ago.

This book also explores the Cape Cod of my youth through another vantage point, that of *The Cape Codder*, a weekly newspaper which came into being in 1946. I took a very enjoyable trip through the early editions to smell and taste the flavor of the Outer Cape, meeting some characters from other towns, and reliving events that had passed from memory.

The Cape Codder of half a century ago was a verbal picture of the Outer Cape, and talks eloquently to us of the times. It was a period when I was coming of age. I knew some of the people in the articles; I certainly knew of the ways of all of them. What seems peculiar behavior now was commonplace then. At the beginning of each part of this book, I relate several *Cape Codder* articles—some paraphrased, some in their entirety. These articles provide some perspective and a colorful backdrop to my own memories, and I thank *The Cape Codder* for allowing me to use them.

Life in Chatham at that time was not all that different from life in the same period in other Cape towns.

It was delightful.

Dana Eldridge

Cape Cod Lucky

In Another Time

Part I
Coming of Age

The Cape Codder Newspaper

In reading the very early editions of the paper, the small town flavor I had experienced was joyously evident right from the start. This item is from a February 8, 1948 issue:

> Alvin Taylor lost two valuable steers out of his herd of thirty last Wednesday afternoon when a group of them broke through the ice on Harvey's Pond. Eight broke through altogether—one drowned, another died from exposure, and a third was in serious condition. Taylor was in the water up to his armpits, pulling steers out by a rope. Both the police and fire departments came to his aid. The steers were in the water for at least half an hour.
>
> The steer in serious condition was saved by drink.
>
> Taylor, under prescription of Dr. Jim Leach, scurried soaking wet to Herb Fuller's package store and bought the cheapest fifth of whiskey in the place. The potion was poured down the steer's throat. Reports are that it got as drunk as a steer. But it pulled through the ordeal.
>
> Herb Fuller said: "Looked to me as though Alvin needed that whiskey more than the steer."

Rural, small town life on Cape Cod in the mid-forties still clung to the last remnants of the unhurried life of the nineteenth century. One of the last of the Cape Cod woodsmen was Ginger Eldredge of East Orleans, whose lifelong pursuit of fur bearing animals was related in detail in *The Cape Codder*. The newspaper also took the opportunity to decry the increasing fees that were making his fur trapper's life untenable.

Skunk oil was apparently a local remedy for whatever ailed you. A Rexall drugstore ad from the 1940s proclaimed its virtues. *The Cape Codder* even ran a front-page photograph of an older gentleman, pipe in mouth, holding a bottle of skunk oil; no story, no name, just a picture.

I remember an old-timer, John Eldredge, who trapped skunks for their oil and fur and lived just down the street from my folks' house on Pleasant Street in South Chatham. He was probably the last of his kind in Chatham.

Pat Cahoon of West Chatham was one of the ageless people on the periphery of the lives of us kids, and with a name change could probably have been found on the edge of any small town, then and now. An article about Pat appeared in *The Cape Codder* on August 15, 1946:

> Few people live as close to the Cape Cod elements as Benjamin F. P. Cahoon, who is generally known as Pat Cahoon. His abode is a rickety, slanting shack on the shore of the Oyster River in West Chatham, and only unfinished boarding fends off the big winds of Winter. Pat gets Old Age Assistance, he scratches a little for quahogs and does considerable beachcombing for his winter fuel.
>
> In short, Pat lives as he pleases. He doesn't have any serious worries. We visited him and his dogs and cats on Saturday to see how it is to live without electric lights, refrigerator, radio, automobile and a shave every day. Pat was born in Harwich. Like most of the oldsters he looks forward to his next birthday. He says he will be 67 on his next birthday.

The most exciting adventure of Pat's lifetime was the hurricane of 1944, which he recounted for *The Cape Codder*:

> The big (1944) hurricane took this building and carried it way to the east'ard. Took everything with it. I tell you when the water gets up to your knees at this cot, it's about time to get out. I had to chop my way out that window and the cats went with me. No sir, I never expected to see this place again when I went out. Cost me some money to get the building set back here. Then the blow they called the 'little hurricane' came after that. Didn't seem much different than the first one

to me. Lost everything again. Even lost my pocketbook with seven or eight dollars in it. I hope we are through with these derned hurricanes.

Chatham was reputed to have a latter-day Henry David Thoreau living in its midst. Called a quiet genius, Charles Howard Doane lived alone in a small building on a freshwater marsh in West Chatham. "I don't want nothin'. I don't have nothin'. I don't need nothin'. I have contentment, peace of mind and comfort. I'm happy and satisfied—and that's true," Doane said in a 1947 interview with *The Cape Codder*. A sign on the walk leading to his house read, "Women over 4 and drunks not admitted."

Sadie Pierce of Orleans thought life in the 1890s was the best time of all. Her account was published on August 22, 1946:

> People didn't swim so much. They went bathing, I didn't swim and there were few women who swam in those days. But we had great fun sailboating… I was always a good walker. Mother said I thought nothing of going to Henry Cummings for a spool of thread—three miles there and three miles back. . . Except for a very few improvements such as electricity and our good roads I'd rather go back to the old days. But I know I'm an exception. People are more selfish today. In my day they wanted the other fellow to have a good time. There were no rights of way then. People used to go anywhere, over the fields or along the shore. There is a selfishness about property rights now.

It used to be that a swimming expedition was an occasion. Heavy, all-concealing cotton suits were donned and the trip to the nearest beach was embarked upon. Then, for the ladies at least, it was a matter of wading out a short distance and sitting on the bottom to luxuriate in the near-weightless feeling while immersed in Nantucket Sound's tea-temperature water.

It was also a time to catch up with the latest news from around town with the other ladies. My great-grandmother and some of her friends were bobbing around off Forest Beach in South Chatham, when an unmindful and unknowingly brave horseshoe crab blundered into her ample posterior. She loosened a shriek, probably audible in Chatham, four miles away. She also loosened her false teeth, which flew out in a graceful arc to plop daintily in the waist-deep, murky water. By the time she and her lady friends had again composed themselves, the teeth were nowhere to be found.

When she arrived home, she summoned her son and instructed him to take a quahog rake down to the shore and scratch around to retrieve the errant teeth. Which he did. No one wants to waste a perfectly good set of false teeth.

I've often wondered what Grampa's thoughts were, though, when he saw those shiny white teeth grinning up at him through the water.

Many articles in *The Cape Codder* chronicled the slipping into oblivion of what was becoming known as the bygone trades. There was an intriguing tale about the last known whaler, his occasionally terrifying exploits, and his often monotonous life aboard his small, floating world. His life onboard was an exaggeration of the everyday life of all of us. He was usually bored by the unvarying monotony of shipboard life and occasionally terrified by his close, hazardous encounters with their quarry.

History was validated by these accounts, but the newspaper also chronicled the present in all its robust vigor. Flying, a novelty before the war, was a novelty no longer. It was becoming a business.

The newspaper described men wanting to start flying schools in nearly every town on the Outer Cape. Eastham and Orleans developed airfields, and someone wanted to make a sea plane base in Orleans' Town Cove. Air service was inaugurated between Newark, New Jersey, and Hyannis. After a stint in the Coast Guard, Dick Kelsey took to the air and made a business out of showing us our beautiful land from on high and became an acclaimed aerial photographer.

Other returning servicemen started businesses. In 1946 Frank Sargent, Willis Gould, and Fred MacFarlane opened a sporting goods store, the Goose Hummock Shop, on the edge of Orleans' Town Cove. It's still doing business at the same stand half a century later. The veterans grabbed for their dreams and made the most of them.

World War ll stimulated the development of technology. One of the seeming wonders was DDT. The early issues of *The Cape Codder* proclaimed how this miracle substance could protect our foliage, kill our pesky wood ticks, and do away with the annoying mosquitoes that made outdoor life so miserable in the summer evenings. Ironically, in the same time period that DDT was being lauded, another article mentioned that conservation was lax in Massachusetts.

There were many headlines back then that would raise an eyebrow or two in any newspaper today:
- Whale Ashore—Blubber Tried Out in Chatham (January 30,1947)
- Eastham Three Holer Stolen, Owner Outraged (August 19, 1948)
- The Best Steaks on a Blackfish (August 26, 1948)

But some of the headlines found in the old papers would read much the same today:
- Brewster Acts to Stop Erosion (February 28, 1946)
- First Bass Caught (May 9, 1947)
- Brewster Herring Run is Big and Started (April 9, 1948)

Then too, a few of the headlines were glimpses into our future:
- Chatham Opposes State Control of Hardings Beach (February 21, 1946)
- Yacht Club Building on Town Cove (March 11, 1948)
- T. V. for Cape Cod? (June 3, 1948)
- Monomoy Land Grab (July 7, 1948)

Few ads for services included phone numbers, yet phones, while not universal, were common. There were very few real estate ads, and the want ads could be counted on the fingers of one hand. The winding down of the world war brought with it changes in our lives, and in our way of life. Changes that still resonate today. The past, that slow-moving, casual, familiar way of life was about to be eclipsed.

Eldridges and Nickersons

I have thirteen generations of Cape Codders on both sides of my family looking over my shoulder. I feel I am fully qualified to reveal a little-known fact about some Cape Codders.

Beneath the solemn exterior, behind the facade of earnestness, some Cape Codders harbor a secret. That is, they have a streak of the unexpected in them, particularly the Nickersons. As a rule they are nice enough, but somewhere not too far buried in their souls, runs a counter-current of the wackies.

My mother is a Nickerson. Unlike the cagey Eldridges, who rarely put anything on paper, the Nickersons kept pretty fair accounts of their doings. We know what the previous generations did on their way to the present.

Consider the first Nickerson, William, who arrived here with his wife and children in 1636. What kind of a man was he to leave all the civilization he had ever known? To know beyond a shadow of a doubt that never again would he rest his eyes on the land of his birth or his relatives? To face a future as uncertain as it was possible to be? Does this sound like the actions of a sane man? To my Eldridge genes it doesn't. The idea of leaving home and hearth sounds insane, wacky. Something my Eldridge side would never consider.

But my Nickerson genes can easily see the spirit of adventure in the endeavor. This aspect of my being would probably jump at the same chance he took. It would be uncertain and adventuresome, something the Nickerson half would embrace wholeheartedly.

William's son, another William, born in what is now Chatham, left his home and his bride to fight against King Philip's warriors in Narragansett's Swamp. The spirit of adventure, the thirst for thrills, called him away from family and safety.

The fourth William, while out duck hunting one cold winter's day, dared a raging tidal creek and lost. His ability was not equal to his daring.

The fifth generation's Stephen joined the Gorham Rangers in the taking of Louisburg in 1745, and came back to the Cape to marry his cousin, Dorcas Nickerson. But that famous Nickerson wanderlust held sway. Soon after returning to the bucolic Cape, he went back to the Provinces to spend the rest of his days, another victim of the lust for excitement.

The second Stephen fought in the Revolutionary War in 1775. He came home to the Cape to become a sailor, then captain and owner of various vessels trading up and down the east coast. Time had not diluted the gene for the high spirited life.

His son, Seth, followed the sea as well; he was captain of the *Orentes*, a trading schooner, and during the War of 1812 was a successful blockade runner. Apparently no timid soul he, either.

One of his sons was Warren, a shipmaster before the age of twenty-one. His *Morning Star* was a coastal trading vessel that called Pleasant Bay home. The wanderlust was still running strong in the gene pool.

His son, my great-grandfather, another Warren, was the district schoolmaster until his hungry children needed a more munificent income to keep them fed. Like so many others of his time he turned to the sea. He became a cod-fisherman out of Pleasant Bay. After some years he probably realized he couldn't fish all his life. He took a chance on the newly developed cranberry culture and soon made that his sole occupation. More evidence of that slightly irrational, "don't play it safe" streak that runs delightfully down through the Nickerson side of the family.

My grandfather had the same adventuresome spirit as all the other Nickersons; he was part of the crew of one of the last of the sailing schooners, an undertaker, and a gifted writer. He also enjoyed a reputation as a competent archaeologist well versed in Cape Cod history. Obviously this man was not stuck in any rut.

Such is the Nickerson side of my family. The Eldridge side is much more controlled and predictable. Their attributes are solid, steady, sometimes stubborn: people who make good shipmates, people you can count on. But as I noted earlier, the Eldridge side didn't keep good records of their doings. We really have no idea what those generations did along the way. Horse thieves or saints, we don't know. Perhaps it's just as well.

In 1945 the Cape's soul was firmly rooted in the past. Every adult over the age of forty clearly remembered their childhood when the horse and buggy was the only form of local transportation. Nana and Grampa Eldridge had a horse and buggy when they were first married, but they bought the first car in Chatham, and Nana lived to see a man walk on the moon. People remembered when cows in the back lot produced milk, the ever-present chickens were a source of eggs, and the older birds became roast and tough chicken for Sunday's dinner. The family garden supplied the vegetables and also a place to get rid of the euphemistically called "dressings," the after-products of those cows and chickens.

But by 1945 the backyard cows had largely given way to the daily milk truck, although one of my friends still went "cross lots" to South Harwich to pick up milk from the last of the small dairy farmers. Horses once used as a means of transportation had long since been retired to greener pastures with one local exception—Abbie Doughnuts, who still hitched up the old horse to go the few miles to the Sou-Wester to quaff a beer or two.

Most families, but not all, had one car and felt lucky to have that. A few people still kept chickens (we did) and some people had a small garden plot (we did) for the fresh and delicious vegetables the thin Cape soil could produce. We went to the shore each fall to collect the washed-up seaweed/salt hay to spread as mulch. We went to the dump each fall for the firewood there for the taking.

At mid-century, debt was a sinful thing: to charge something and not pay for it was to admit you couldn't manage your own affairs. Everything was bought with cash, even cars. If you didn't have the money you didn't get the goods. People that couldn't meet their bills were somehow looked down upon, particularly if they weren't working flat out at whatever came along. To have work was to have respect in the community.

Telephones were fairly common but not universal. In those days telephones were a primary connection to people. Operators were there when you picked up the phone. There were no mind-numbing menus, no interminable "Please holds," just a pleasant voice asking, "Number, please."

I can still remember my grandmother's number: #139, Ring 3. She was on a party line. When it was her call, her phone would ring three times. This sounds cumbersome and it probably was. But there was a real social benefit to this arrangement. The same operator who took your request could often find the party you were trying to reach. She (and it was always a she) knew who was visiting whom, where the people in town were, and if the need was urgent, would track down the person you were trying to reach.

One of the drawbacks of a party line was that anyone could listen in on any of the calls on that line. But not everyone considered that a drawback. Before the days of canned entertainment, the party line was the semi-public pulse on the local doings. An example of this community service occurred just down the street, just a few houses away from my grandmother's home.

Mercy was of my grandmother's generation and one of the brightest ladies in town. Perhaps because of her brightness and her husband's lack of same, she was terribly lonely. She, like a lot of women of her era, didn't drive. Her only excursions were via the telephone, the old party line. Her false teeth didn't fit all that well. Her asthmatic breath whistled a bit as she became excited. She was, in short, an audible listener. A listener that was all too obvious on our party line. Most of the time she was tolerated as she eavesdropped, but occasionally, when the subject was too personal to share, the command would be given, "Whoever is listening in, please hang up." Inevitably a soft click would be the answer. Everyone knew who the eavesdropper was; the clicking teeth and raspy breath left little doubt. The "whoever" was just to maintain the facade of innocence when the caller ran into Mercy at the post office.

Everyone knew about Mercy's circumstances and tolerated her behavior. The tolerance and the understanding were a commonsense way of tacitly helping a needy neighbor. This was the very essence of small town living.

We lived on Pleasant Street, a short distance south of Route 28 which ran right through the little town. My Eldridge grandparents lived on Route 28, an easy half-mile or so away. Sometimes I wonder just how many of my grandmother's fork-marked peanut butter cookies I devoured, how many molasses cookies I slid into my cookie-crumbed pockets. I'm sure it was thousands of each kind and there wasn't a bad one in the bunch.

Her gingerbread, the best I've ever eaten, was of an unknown variety—thick, heavy, with a crinkled crust and a sprinkling of sugar on top, fudgelike in consistency and wonderfully delicious. I've never tasted anything like that gingerbread since and that's a great pity.

In their large house lived Nana and Grampa, his mother (Little Nana), her mother and father (Gramma and Grandpa Bearse), and my two adult uncles. Today, such arrangements are rare at best. Back then, it was just the way it was. Today, if it happened at all, it would be called an extended family; back then, it was just a warm, friendly place where someone was almost always home and welcome was certain. This comfortable house was the friendliest in a very friendly small town.

But friendly or not, the occasional fracas created a need for at least a token police force. In 1945 Chatham had three all but invisible policemen. Only the Chief was full time. There was no official police car. The Chief's car served double duty, both as his family car and also as the town's official car. Apparently that was all that was needed; (only 782 cars were registered in Chatham in 1945, over 10,000 in 1999). It appears in that time of global crisis, crime was a minor aspect of town living.

Generally everyone got along. The force, such as it was, was respected. Usually common sense prevailed in our sparsely populated community. Occasionally, when tempers ran high (and this was a rare occurrence), the Chief would be called in to mediate. Because this man was well respected, his pronouncement was usually the end of the fracas.

But in some respects the Cape was not all that different from our more populous neighbors, Boston and New York. Someone was always on the lookout to separate money from the gullible.

My father and two others decided to buy an old, thirty-foot trap boat that was offered for a very low price. The seller's reputation left a lot to be desired, that is, he was well known as a sharp dealer. Sharp in that he and the word "ethics" were not well acquainted.

Undeterred by wifely warnings about this shady character, my father and the other two men went ahead with the transaction. At the price (a total of eighty hard-earned dollars), they felt they couldn't go wrong.

The boat was blocked up down on the shore of Stage Harbor. It needed a lot of work (all old wooden boats did), but it was functional and with a paint job and some patching it would work out just fine for a number of years. The three of them went right to work, scraping, sanding, and painting. Later in the spring during these weekend projects, they noticed that a local fish buyer (who had been down south all winter) was checking their progress quite regularly. He would stop and talk over the job, congratulate them on the good work they were doing, and remark how handsome the old boat looked. As the work neared completion, his attentions became more noticeable, almost as though he had a proprietary interest in the project. He was still as genial as ever, still seemingly impressed with the work they were doing. When the last seam was caulked and the last coat of paint slapped on, the now sharp-looking craft was ready to be launched. Again, the fish buyer was on hand, but this time he had a question.

"What are you fellas going to do with the old boat?"

They replied, " We thought we'd use it to fish the rips, weekend trips with the families, that kind of thing. First though, we have to find a mooring to hang it on."

"That's no problem at all boys, hang it on my mooring out there off the pier. As a matter of fact that's where it belongs. This is my boat."

It seems the boat seller, knowing that the boat owner was in Florida for the winter, had seen a thirst for boat ownership in some greenhorns and didn't let the fact he didn't own the craft get in the way of the transaction.

It also seemed the boat owner, understanding the situation, had had his boat scraped, sanded, and painted for nothing.

Eventually the three erstwhile buyers decided to take the seller to court in an attempt to get their $80 back. The embarrassment of being snookered by a local disreputable character—that was something they would have to learn to live with.

When the court date came up, my ever-thrifty father called the police chief and wondered if he could hitch a ride to the courthouse in Harwich Center. The Chief had to go right by the house anyway, and if he could catch a ride, it would let my mother have the car for the day, a rare treat for her.

"No problem, Wib, we'll pick you up around ten."

Wib never thought to ask who the "we'll" referred to.

When the Chief's car pulled up, there were four men already in it: the Chief, Wib's two partners, and the boat seller. It must have been a cramped ride to the courthouse.

I've often wondered what they talked about on their ride to the halls of justice, and particularly on the way back after the judgement went against the boat seller. Knowing the normal parsimonious speech of these men, I doubt if a syllable was uttered. I don't think they ever did get all their money back either.

There is a postscript to this story.

About forty years later, my father discovered his outboard wasn't swinging on its mooring out front, as usual. Summer's ever-present southwest wind had had its way with the mooring line, chafed it through, and had deposited the boat high, dry, and unscathed on the beach, a half-mile or so distant, but in plain sight from the house. Wib knew there was no hurry in retrieving the craft, that he might as well wait for the high tide to lift her off the shore. Then he could wander down the beach to bring it back. Not much could happen to it in the meantime.

He checked the tideline from time to time to keep an eye on the water creeping up to the high-and-dry boat. He wanted to be there when she lifted off.

But apparently Wib wasn't the only one checking the tidelines that day. About the time he was ready to saunter down the beach to retrieve the errant boat he noticed someone had arrived on the scene ahead of him.

Wib was stimulated (and this was not a word commonly associated with this most deliberate of men) into hasty action. He put on his boots and hurried down the shore. Coming off the beach was the same boat seller of four decades earlier, laden down with life preservers, fish poles, gas tanks—all he could carry of the paraphernalia found in any boat.

Caught dead to rights in his effort to liberate the boat's gear, his ingenious, smiling explanation was, "Hi there, Wib, here's your gear. I was just saving it for ya. Didn't want anyone to take it."

Apparently the details of ownership had not weighed heavily on his mind in the intervening forty years.

Don't "Let On"

Cape Codders have a deserved reputation for not "letting on." They will take considerable pains to carefully conceal any feelings that may intrude in their lives. It's as though telling how they feel, by showing enthusiasm or sadness, will somehow diminish their character, as if they will give something precious away. Good feelings, terrible feelings, it doesn't matter: Cape Codders don't want to let on. And they rarely do.

I don't know why the old Cape Codders were this way. Maybe they thought openness of expression equated to the open seams of the wooden boats that most of them used to have. Wooden boats with open seams sink. Perhaps the old-timers saw openness in expression as leading to a similar unpleasant result. More likely this "not letting on" was a pragmatic way of dealing with the unexpected, the bumps in life we all experience. In that era, in that time, it probably never occurred to them to mention these bumps or the high spots. They just dealt with them and moved on. Life didn't wait.

Not wanting to make a fuss, "not letting on," as far as I was concerned, was carried a bit too far one hot summer afternoon. I was delivering newspapers and as usual, burst into my grandparents' house on the run via the road-side sun porch door. The tables on the porch, which were used for winter storage and rarely had anything on them, now sported a long, lumpy object, covered with an old, worn, red-checkered oilcloth. Never had I seen anything covered like that. My eyes traveled the length of the lumps and came to rest on two scuffed shoes sticking out from under the oilcloth.

There was little question of what lay under that shape-revealing covering. At least my head knew; my heart didn't want to know. I knew it wasn't either of my grandparents; the shape was all wrong. I later learned it was the result of a motorcycle going too fast across a patina of sand on the curve of Route 28 out front. The medical examiner, Doc Keene, a very pragmatic man, didn't want the body to spoil lying out in the sun, so they brought him in on the shady sun porch to await the hearse. I had come in, as I always did, by that road-side sun porch door. I left by the kitchen door, hurriedly, and ever after I checked those sun porch tables before I came running in.

This casual and commonsense way of dealing with a problem was typical of the mores of the day. No fuss, no hysteria, just an acceptance of the conditions and a measured response. "Don't let on" at its finest.

Another measured response occurred in South Orleans between Big and Little Bay, where Pleasant Bay nips in its waist and generates good fishing.

Uncle Bob and I were at this spot, called the Narrows, one early fall evening. The boat was anchored and we were drifting eels, hoping to catch a few big stripers. The stars were putting on their usual autumnal array. There wasn't a breath of air. Way off in the distance though, we heard the faint buzz of a tiny motor. Over time this sound grew louder and louder until finally, after half an hour or so, a large, ponderous-looking skiff, powered by a very small outboard, loomed out of the darkness.

"You fellah's got any?" was the lone occupant's query.

"One," was the answer.

"Huh, that ain't many," he replied, and back into the darkness droned the small motor with the small talker.

For the next half hour we chuckled as we listened to the tiny motor's slowly diminishing sound as the verbally parsimonious, utterly normal, Cape Codder headed home. He probably had regretted it wasn't daylight, when the entire paltry conversation could have been carried on with no words at all, just gestures.

At age sixteen I found myself emulating this "don't let on" behavior, and now I wonder why.

At my beloved Grandfather's funeral no one cried. They all cared deeply for this wonderful man; he had died prematurely and no one (including me) let on that it was a very sad thing. I was young and it was the very first funeral I had ever attended. I kept checking to see when it was okay to cry and it never was, though I desperately wanted to. A huge, happy piece of my life was gone forever and it hurt, it hurt a lot.

No one I saw at the well-attended church service "let on." Just a few sniffles, a few dabs by small hankies, that was it. He was gone as if he had never existed and he had done so much for so many people. I never knew why the attendees showed so little emotion. It was just the way people were in those days in that village. Life didn't wait for Grampa, either.

But not all the lessons I was learning about life were as soul shattering. Some were perplexing and in retrospect, funny. Then it was normal behavior, nothing worth commenting on. At my first-ever regular job, I worked twenty hours a week at a local gas station and junk yard. The owner, Chicky Clark, was as nice as could be, but a talker he was not. . During the course of the summer I don't think he said a total of more than a few hundred words to his usually bewildered apprentice.

My father (Wib), a classmate of Chicky's in the Chatham schools, was raised in the same tradition. Maybe it went with the schooling they received. Maybe it had something to do with the water they drank. Whatever the cause, Wib, too, was anything but a loquacious man.

When Wib stopped in at Chicky's to get some gas he would hold up two dollars (eight gallons). Chicky would grunt, but just a little, pump the gas, take the bills, and head back into his station. There were no hard feelings, no animosity, just no words. And these were two men that had known each other all their lives in the very small town we lived in.

My great-uncle Oscar Nickerson was a ship captain at twenty-one, and it should be mentioned that the life of a ship captain allowed for little time ashore. Those rare times at home were treasured and sometimes frustrating.

On one of his visits home, he and his wife went to the Harwich Exchange Hall for a performance. After the show, when the attendees were exchanging comments and hitching up their horses, Oscar's wife, Eglatine, noticed that Oscar seemed to be delaying their departure, something quite unusual for him. When she queried him about his hesitancy, all she got in response was a grunt. She thought more about it and finally realized that her husband was home so rarely he didn't know his own horse. Oscar was waiting for the other men to select their steeds. The one that was left was bound to be his. He just didn't want to "let on" that he was a stranger to his own livestock. Ship captains didn't have to explain their actions to anyone.

This habit of not letting on has run through the generations of Cape Codders since time began. But these well-hidden feelings aren't totally in eclipse, they are just very well hidden.

On September 2, 1945, these all-but-eclipsed emotions were brought to the fore and amply displayed right on the Main Street of Chatham.

There were men and women cavorting, dancing, and laughing in the streets in the full glare of headlights that had been dimmed for the past four years. There were at least a hundred or so onlookers, and they too were joining in the gaiety, right there in front of the Mayflower Shop. What had happened to the stoic people of my town? Harold Tuttle, a cousin, was right there with all the rest, arms all akimbo, dancing in wild abandon, singing right along. I didn't know adults could or would sing and dance right out in the open. It was a happy mob scene and a most unusual sight for the main street of Chatham anytime in my life. I couldn't help but wonder if we had somehow blundered into some strange, previously hidden, very lively section of town. And in that era, mentioning Chatham and lively in the same sentence would have been an oxymoron of the highest order.

The fact that we were in Chatham at all was also unusual. Chatham was five miles from our home in South Chatham, and we seldom went into town and never in the evening. There was gas rationing, and we didn't do those kinds of frivolous things during the war years and rarely ever in the best of times.

The word was out that Japan had surrendered, and Chatham's people were celebrating. The long, anxiety-fraught war was finally over. In Chatham alone, 300 of our uncles, cousins, family, and friends had been in harm's way and all but three were soon to be headed home.

For me, at the age of fourteen, the fact that the war was over was less of a surprise (it had been a foregone conclusion for some time) than the fact that Chathamites were cavorting in plain sight. The bottled-up emotions I had grown up with were nowhere evident that night. Had a tidal wave come up Main Street it would have been no less surprising. On reflection though, it was a tidal wave—a tidal wave of joy that Chathamites happily surrendered to. After fifteen years of global unrest (conditions we Cape Codders did little to cause and could do little about), the world was back on a hopeful track. A cause for celebration indeed.

The Great Depression had little effect on Cape Cod. Few families had any great amounts of money to lose; Wall Street with its boom and bust cycles was something that happened somewhere over the bridge.

World War II, however, had a major effect. Very few families escaped the avaricious, searching tentacles of global conflict. Our families had been diminished, some for the duration, a few forever, and our resources had been strained to the limit. During the war, a trip down any road in Chatham revealed windows hung with the little flags that had a white background and a blue star symbolizing a son or daughter in the service and the occasional gold star indicating the family's ultimate sacrifice.

But as the war wound down, I think we all thought that life would get back to a semblance of normalcy. And it did for awhile, but only for a short period. Unlike the pre-war times, normalcy was no longer static. Normalcy now was change.

Change—All Change

Our young men and women had seen the world, seen other cultures. Our nation's people now knew we could do anything we set our minds to. We had surmounted the Great Depression, and without exaggeration, we had saved the world from tyranny. The nation's miasma of hopelessness during the decade or more of the depression years, plus the uncertainty and sacrifice of the four years of the global war was banished. Despair was replaced with joy, hopelessness was replaced with hopefulness.

Soon after the war, the interstate road system, coupled with reliable cars, put all of the continent within anyone's reach. There was money to spend on leisure, something that had been in short supply before and during the war, and now there were places to go.

For the half of the nation's population that lived in the northeast within a day's drive of Cape Cod's magnificent beaches, that seemed to translate into "head for those beaches" every summer. And Cape Codders, one of our nation's pockets of parochial peoples, were about to undergo a sea change.

The bucolic Outer Cape, dozing quietly for nearly all the first half of the century, awoke with a start. More people than we ever thought possible were at the gates. The old unwritten rules no longer applied. Sons didn't necessarily follow in their father's footsteps. Fishing and farming were no longer the linchpins of the Cape's economy. Postwar Cape Codders found jobs parceling out real estate and in building and construction. Getting used to their new neighbors was to be their avocation.

Cape Cod Lucky

Cape Cod reeled under the impact of increased tourism. The limitations of our country roads and small parking lots at the beaches began to tell. Soon the arguments surfaced: should we improve (widen and enlarge) our roads and beach parking to accommodate the throngs? Or should we let the poor roads and small parking lots remain as they are to act as basic traffic controls? These arguments resound today in much the same way, fueled by the same conflicting forces.

New roads brought a new breed of tourist to the Cape. Prior to the war it was common for families to come for the summer, with the head of the household returning (by train) for the weekends, as our next-door neighbors, the Masseys, did. All that changed with the easier access provided by the automobile. Postwar visitors came for shorter periods, often splitting their vacation time between the mountains in the winter and the sea during the summer's inviting weather.

For a surprisingly long period after the war, land remained inexpensive here on the Cape. At one point in the late thirties my grandfather told me he would give some of his land away if he knew anyone that would take it. The desire for a cottage on the Cape was easily matched by the desire of Cape Codders to unload land that had been, in many cases, a tax burden for years.

Builders moved here from off-Cape to take advantage of the many building opportunities. The woods came down, houses went up. The Cape was changing right before our eyes and we were all part of that change.

Our family was a microcosm of all that was going on in the transformation that was changing the face and flavor of the Cape. All of the men in my family in the generation preceding mine had been involved in the global conflict; one in the Pacific, one in Europe, and one here on the Cape. This is not to disparage the work of the wives of these men. Their contributions were, by necessity, limited. There was little gas, no one had a second car, and there was no public transportation. What these hard-working women did had to be done at home or close by.

After the war these same men were somehow involved in serving the needs of the newly mobile folks of the rest of the nation that wanted to share this lovely peninsula. One was a builder, one a house painter, and one worked in the banking business.

For another decade or so after the war's end, my contemporaries and I were able to enjoy an awakening Cape Cod in a manner few, if any, of the generations before us had ever done. We had a little extra cash, plenty of time, and a largely unpopulated landscape to enjoy. For the generations coming along after us it was to be another story.

The Cape of my youth was a Cape bounded only by the physical boundaries of geography, our endurance, and our imagination—a Cape that was enjoyed to the hilt for those of us who lived here. For the fortunate few of us born during the Great Depression, life has only been getting better with each passing year. We were born in a period that is now defined as desperate times, a time of deprivation for the nation. But here on the Cape, no one sold apples on the street corner, no one jumped out of tall buildings (it wouldn't have been much of a jump, there weren't any tall buildings). The only people that were jumping, jumped on the flats to make the clams squirt and thereby, easier to find. The meals may have been repetitious, but they were also nutritious, and we never felt the scourge of hunger. Being brought up in such conditions is not arduous. We knew nothing else. We always had enough to eat, we always slept in a warm house, we were sheltered and succored by our families and the numerous relatives living all around us. Very few outside influences intruded in our lives. Our benchmarks were ourselves and the past generations' achievements. For nearly all of Cape Cod's children growing of age in that time, life was not in any sense difficult.

One of the first intimations we kids had that our Cape was changing hit hard one hot July evening, when a few of us decided to have a swim at the obliging Goose Pond, something we frequently did. On this particular evening though, the thin edge of the wedge of change curtailed and dampened our plans. We had always used the beach, the only white sand beach on the pond. That evening, the beach sported a new sign that on closer examination said, "Private Property. KEEP OUT." This seemed ridiculous to us. Maybe it was someone's idea of a joke. This was the only beach of consequence on the pond. Why shouldn't we use it? There wasn't a living soul in view, only the green woods that had always reigned over this delightful kettle hole pond.

We ignored the sign and had our usual fun time splashing around in those soft, inviting waters.

Suddenly, the author of the dread sign came out of the woods, down on the beach and invited us to vacate ourselves from his beach. Our protestations were to no avail, our queries as to whom we were bothering elicited no response, and most ominous of all was the answer to our question, "Does this mean we can never use this beach again?" That answer was a resounding, "Yes, keep off my beach." Of course we would use it again and again, but only when the "Goose Pond Genghis" wasn't around.

Change, not all of it welcome, was on the way, and we would have to get used to it. We did, and surprisingly came to realize in time that the changes weren't so onerous; that our Cape, while changing, was still enjoyable. The solitude we all needed from time to time was still easy to find; the shellfish we loved were still available and the finfish were still ready to take a lure and delight us both in the catching and in the eating. The ocean still had the grandeur it had always maintained. The fringing white sands were renewed each year ready to delight the beachgoers as they always had.

Best of all, most of the people that were moving here to share that which we had always enjoyed seemed to realize the fragility of this bucolic land. Their persistence and perseverance have outshone most of us natives in their zeal to protect our heritage and our land. It's a bit ironic and altogether fortunate that the change we so feared and despised brought with it the seeds of salvation.

Many of these newcomers had seen first hand what havoc uncontrolled development could wrack on a community. Fortunately for us natives who were reeling from the onslaught, the newcomers saw the need for government control as the only tool to stop development. The trade-off for the unpleasant aspect of government ownership of our land is the very pleasant reality that approximately 30,000 acres of the Outer Cape has been put out of the reach of developers for all time. It is held in trust for all of us and ours as a National Seashore. The plethora of "No Trespassing" signs and the roads and houses that are proliferating all over the Cape will be held in abeyance on these lands.

And a bit about the Cape's own approximation of the devil: the mighty Atlantic, which gives with one hand and takes away a little more than it gives with the other. It at once gives us our flavor, our essence, our soul, and in the giving, it is taking the very firmament that is Cape Cod.

There is a river of sand flowing unabated down our eastern flank, an event we can do very little about except bear witness to our own demise. Every year here on the Outer Cape, on average, about three-and-a-half feet of that forty-mile stretch of cliff face slides off into the devouring Atlantic. Every century, about 500 acres are gone forever. What was upland is now shallow saltwater, good for fishing, but not good to stand on. What frozen water brought, liquid water is reclaiming.

The students of coastal geology tell us the erosion patterns can be likened to a giant garden hose directed at the "wrist" of the Cape, somewhere in the Truro area. Apparently, at this point, some minor currents swing north to carry sand in a generally westerly and later southerly direction, which makes the "clenched fist" of Provincetown. The major currents, however, move from Truro south along the entire outer, eastern shore of Cape Cod. This long shore current isn't doing the Cape any favors. Sand moves easily; sand driven by the wind and water moves very easily.

I've read Cape Cod has the second highest average wind velocity (15 miles per hour) in the country. Having lived here most of my life I can believe that's true. That south-tending, longshore current coupled with the wind-driven waves is moving our real estate out to sea. The prognosis can't be good if you live on the coast and the only bedrock is sand.

An onshore wind—the easterlies, often of magnificent proportions—slams into the Cape and we all rush to see the mighty surf. It's quite a sight, one we look at with awe, thinking how nice it is to be sitting in the warm, comfortable car and not having to be out in that turbulent, roiling water fighting for our very survival.

We wonder at the strength of those waves as they batter the gently sloping beach again and again. Those waves, with the rising tide, undercut and collapse the cliffs that face the writhing Atlantic. The collapsing cliffs stain the white froth a dirty orange-yellow, as an epitaph to mark their passing. After a week or so in the bosom of the ocean those yellow sands become the familiar white sands of the Outer Cape. Lying on these warm white sands on any glorious summer day is always a delight, but we are lying on new sand that has been untouched since its glacial arrival approximately twenty thousand years ago. And next year, when we again lay on that same beach, it will be on more new sand. Last year's sand will be somewhere south of us and very likely out at sea. We are riding a shrinking, sinking ship, albeit sinking very slowly. It's a sinking probably no one can stop. We can't stop the wind, the ocean is rising faster than ever, and the rock base we need to hold the ocean at bay isn't here.

Our architect, the glacier, didn't see fit to bring many rocks to shore up our bulwarks. In fact, our substantial rocks are so few and far between we often name them, perhaps in the forlorn hope that by naming them they, and maybe ourselves, will achieve some permanence. I wonder if someone could get in touch with the ghost of the bygone glaciers and suggest it go back for a good solid load of rocks for our tenuous eastern flank. Those long ago glaciers did a good job of making this peninsula such a delightful place to live; it seems such a shame to watch it all slide into the sea.

And so it has been for all the 15,000-20,000 years the Cape has been extant. So it has been all my life.

Knowing of the ocean's relentless advance doesn't make it any less picturesque. For the summer throngs or the hardy winter beach walkers, the glorious ocean doesn't lack for lookers. Any day of the year, any time of day, someone is at the shore looking over those limitless miles of always moving water. Like a fireplace fire the ocean's attraction is universal. Wherever there are parking lots close to the ocean a steady procession of people will come to view, to get a spiritual sip of ocean to tide them over until their next visit.

The Cape's relationship to the omnipotent ocean is multifaceted. The sea destroys the land but is also a medium that supports life year round. While we bemoan the inevitable advance of the unstoppable ocean we also enjoy what it offers so liberally.

Dolphins are just one of nature's liberal offerings just waiting for us to savor. In my youth, these sleek mammals were common in the food rich waters of Nantucket Sound. Summer Sunday rides in the old catboat used to provide us a close-hand look at the grinning faces of those bow riders. It must have been dull fare for those lithe animals, slogging along with the old boat, maybe going five miles an hour, while they were easily capable of speeds far in excess of our ploddings. I can clearly remember lying on that minuscule foredeck watching the alert eyes of those intelligent creatures just a foot or two away looking back at me. I wondered what they were thinking, why they were riding our sluggish bow wave, and why they always appeared to be grinning. But why not grin? Life was easy, food was plentiful, and all sorts of playthings were in the water, including an occasional old catboat creeping along. From the dolphin's point of view, things couldn't have been better. For us, too.

Fishing

Like dolphins, porpoises and whales used to be common in all Cape waters. My great-uncle Carroll Nickerson saw all of the marine mammals that sported in the Cape's waters. Uncle Carroll was my grandfather's brother, a sailing fisherman all his life. He lived in the old farmhouse which is now part of the Wequasset complex overlooking Round Cove, just off Pleasant Bay.

I was just a young boy when Uncle Carroll was finishing up his life, but I still clearly remember his stories of how the whales migrating up and down the coast would come around his boat, most of them longer and far heavier than his little craft. He told of the stench of their breath and how they never bothered him, though they often passed close enough to touch with an oar.

Uncle Carroll was one of the last of the sailing fishermen. He never did put an engine in his beloved *Gladys*, a twenty-four-foot catboat. His life was winding down when engines were becoming reliable enough to revolutionize boat propulsion. He stuck with what he knew best, and those sails and his skill served him well. So well, that an article in the July, 1953 issue of *Yachting* magazine describes him as "enjoying the undisputed reputation of being the most skillful catboat skipper on Cape Cod."

I well remember going over to their Round Cove home for Sunday visits. Aunt Emmie always had a dish of ice cream and kind words for me. Uncle Carroll was a ramrod straight man with no hair and the most marvelous goatee—an imposing and yet somehow kindly figure. With the weathered tan and twinkling, bleached-blue eyes of a lifetime on the water, his demeanor and his stance personified "Captain." He also had a reputation for brooking no nonsense on his boat.

A family story tells of his refusing to take Joe Lincoln out on his *Gladys*. At that time Mr. Lincoln was a popular, nationally known author and raconteur. Many of the characters in his books were caricatures of old Cape Codders speaking in an exaggerated accent. Uncle Carroll had no intention of showing up on the pages of some book as another yokel from the Cape.

The fishermen of those times would get started before dawn and sail out of Pleasant Bay over the Roaring Bull (Chatham Bars) to the fishing grounds off Chatham, five to twenty miles distant, the trip timed to catch the slack tide on the grounds. Then it was fish all day standing up (you can't sit down to jig for cod) in a constantly moving, shifting boat. By mid-afternoon it was up sail and head for home. And with prevailing Westerly wind, it was often an upwind sail, half of the time against the tide. Once the bar was crossed, the slog up the bay made, and the boat finally moored, the drudgery began.

In those days refrigeration was not an option and a boatload of fish on a warm July evening wouldn't interest a cat the next morning. The codfish had to be pitchforked from the catboat into the dory and rowed near shore.

A gore-besplattered table was dragged off the beach into the water, a lantern hung, and each fish was handled once again, to be gutted, washed, and smeared with salt. They were then restacked in the dory for their final waterborne journey ashore.

Such was the life of one of the Cape's "Codfish Aristocracy" as told by my Uncle Carrol's brother, my grandfather, Warren Sears Nickerson, in his book, *The Bay as I See It*.

"What a sight it must have been in deep dusk on the bay's edge, the yellow guttering lantern with various bits of smoking fish flesh sticking to its hot chimney, the tired men working under the lash of a spoiling catch. On a calm night the buzzing of the multitudes of mosquitos would be all but deafening. At their feet the eels and the night creatures sinuously waiting for something good to fall from the table, waiting for their share of the spoils. And somewhere not so far away, the good wife too, waiting dinner for her man."

And these men went fishing year round. Uncle Carroll relates coming in reefed down as far as she would go, boiling in over the Roaring Bull, riding a bitter cold, boisterous northeast wind, the catboat's boom looking like a comb for the giants, the comb's teeth, foot-long icicles. These men were tough and they excelled at a tough job.

The men who worked these waters knew where the dangers lay and they well knew how to circumvent them. For offshore work, the compass, the clock, and a thorough knowledge of the currents and bottoms would put the fisherman on his favorite grounds with surprising accuracy.

One story has it that to test their captain's uncanny knowledge of the sea bottom around Nantucket, a whale ship crew took along a bucketful of soil from their good captain's garden. As the ship cleared Great Point in black fog and struck off to the sou'ard, the captain ordered a sounding and a bottom sample. Over the side went the tallow-coated sounding lead to pick up a sample of bottom material. The crew made a great to-do about hauling it in and in a high state of feigned excitement they brought the lead (after rubbing it thoroughly in the garden soil) to the captain to examine. He, of the uncanny knowledge, rose to the challenge:

"Come about boys, for Lord's sakes come about! We have to get back. From the looks of this lead, Nantucket's sunk!"

Earning one's living on the high seas has always been garlanded with an aura of romance. One description of retirees emphasized this aura. It noted that retired bookkeepers don't spend much time looking at adding machines but retired fisherman can often be found down at the docks, watching (and commenting on) the new generation's efforts.

Year after year, the predawn cough and rattle of cold diesel engines coming to life is a sure indication that the end of the cold season has loosened the Chatham fishing fleet. In my youth, the engines were gasoline, but the boats were much the same. These were small boats, under fifty feet, able to go out and return in a day. These boat owners, by choosing Chatham's protected inlets as their harbor, had opted to sleep at home each night.

Anyone at the fish pier an hour or two before dawn on a day with a favorable weather forecast would hear the clatter of reluctant and noisy engines being coaxed into life. He would see the lights coming on in the awakening boats, the last-minute preparations for the eight-to-twelve hour trip being made. This dockside watcher would hear the splash of the mooring line, the rumble of the engines changing to a lower pitch as the boats were put in gear and the parade of lights headed for Chatham Bars.

Chatham Bars (the Roaring Bull of old) is a fearsome shallow spot between the safety of the mooring and the open ocean where the fish are. It is where the often fractious ocean waters meet the more benign waters of Pleasant Bay. This meeting can be wildly turbulent, oily calm, or anything in between. Never does a knowing boatman go over the bar without apprehension, and never does a knowing boatman get over the bar without at least a little sigh of relief.

An extension of these same Chatham Bars all but wiped out the Pilgrims on that November day in 1620, when their sluggish ship, the Mayflower, averaging a speed of slightly less than two miles per hour, was being swept down onto these shallow waters by a brisk northeast breeze. But for a providential and unusual wind shift from the southwest, these early pioneers would have ended their search for religious tolerance in the wild waters off Chatham. These waters and that bar still command respect. Nearly every year the papers tell of boats and people lost when they dare those very real dangers.

Years ago, a local fisherman plying the surfline off North Beach for striped bass dared the crashing waves and lost. His boat rolled over and trapped him under it. Like most fishermen, Wilfred couldn't swim a stroke; the only way he could survive was to hang on to the capsized boat and hope it came ashore before he lost his grip. It wasn't totally dark in the inverted boat; sunlight bouncing off the bottom gave a green-blue, unearthly light that let him assess his grim predicament. His chances were not good.

The only thing keeping him alive was that the upside-down boat was bouncing off the bottom, the shallow waters not letting the vessel sink. But which way was it going: toward deep water or shallow? Toward life or toward death? He knew that if the boat washed into deeper water it would eventually sink with him entombed in the cabin. He knew if it washed up on the beach he would very likely survive.

It's hard to imagine Wilfred's thoughts. Trapped inside a wooden air bubble, he could hear the booming waves crashing against the overturned hull and could feel the hull slew this way and that as those savaging swells knocked the derelict boat about.

The easterly wind coupled with a rising tide buffeted the inverted boat over the outer bar and deposited it on the gently sloping, welcoming sands of North Beach. When the tide went out it left the hulk high and dry.

Wilfred, who had ridden her ashore, dug away the mound of gear blocking the exit, crawled out onto the white sand up to the high beach in the bright sunshine, and marveled at his deliverance. Sometime later, when his rescuers came, he was sitting on the red bottom of the boat exulting in his triumph over the fate that every fisherman dreads.

It must have taken deep reserves of courage to overcome the thoughts that had to have been in his mind when he next rode those massive swells over the bar. He never did learn to swim, and many years later he died peacefully in his bed with his loved ones nearby, helping him on his final voyage over another bar.

Every day possible the fishermen leave harbor heading out to the Lemons, the Pumpkins, the Wrecks, or any of the myriad proven grounds off Chatham, out over the Roaring Bull in their forty- or forty-five-foot power boats.

From the parking lot in front of Chatham Light we can watch them coming back in, their colorful boats looking so small against the vast expanse of that blue sea. Our hearts go out to those men who brave that ocean day after day, toil on its limitless acres, and return home to rest for the next day's effort. It makes the price of fish and lobsters seem quite reasonable.

That fish are found in these waters at all, should come as no surprise—after all, the Cape is named after a fish that was fairly common in its waters. As long as these fish remain fairly common, fishermen will dare the Bars and in their sturdy boats, harvest the pastures of the sea, as man has done since the first fish was brought flapping to the shore by some heavy-browed ancestor of ours.

During the late forties and most of the fifties, one of my uncles was a commercial fisherman out of Chatham. His boat, like most of the rest of the fleet, was a Novi (built in Nova Scotia). These boats were characteristically high bowed and low sterned. They were handsome boats, ideal for the working conditions on Chatham's fishing grounds, and ideal also for dealing with the short steep waves around the Cape's elbow, some of the worst on the Atlantic Coast.

In those days, fishermen were mostly tub trawlers. A trawl is a long-line with hooks every six feet or so. Uncle Bob and his partner, Herb, would get down to the boat a couple hours before dawn, bait each of the thousands of hooks, and set out for one of the fish-rich hot spots. After a day of setting the trawl, retrieving the trawl, and slatting the fish into the bins, it was time for the long slog back to the fish pier. There, the fish got their rudimentary cleaning in preparation for shipment to Boston or New York, where Chatham's fresh fish always commanded a premium price.

When I was invited to go along on one of their trips, I jumped at the chance. Other than being seasick half the time, the trip was fun. On the way in I was asked to steer so the two men could clean the fish. I could barely see over the coaming, but my job was easy. Just follow the compass heading. With no land in sight to distract me, Uncle Bob must have figured I couldn't get into too much trouble.

A slab of black reared out of the water right in front of us. It was my first near acquaintance with a whale. The sleek, glistening black back came up out of the featureless ocean like a surfacing submarine, perpendicular to the boat's course. I yanked the wheel hard over to avoid a collision and precipitated a nice little round of profanity. My sharp, unexpected turn had deposited my uncle in one of the fish boxes and all but sent Herb overboard.

"What in the merry hell do you think you are doing?"

I tried to explain that we had been about to run down a whale and that I had saved us from a collision. All to no effect. I was told to steer the compass course and unless threatened by the Queen Mary herself not to deviate by so much as a degree. The whales would take care of themselves.

When we arrived at dockside the unloading began. The fish were forked into tubs, hoisted over the caplog, and dumped all splattery and slimy into a chute to be sorted for shipment to the waiting markets.

One summer day, Eben, a truck driver with a well-deserved reputation as a hell-raiser, was waiting at the pier for his fish truck to be loaded. This was a boring time for Eben. It took hours for all the boats to unload, hours to hatch some scheme to while away the time. The pier in those days had no observation deck. The fisherman and the tourists alike milled about on the same dock. The signs asking the tourists to stay back were largely ignored. They were underfoot and grudgingly tolerated, but they were also fair game for any accidental "flying fish."

The unloading was a common enough sight. The boats would come in against the pier and make fast. The fishermen would then pitchfork the fish into the lowered bins. Once full, the bins would be hoisted over the caplog and the fish spilled down the chutes to be sorted. It was a sight that Eben had seen hundreds of times and which evoked a need in him for a more lively response.

Somewhere, he had come across an unwanted, blue baby carriage. Eben lashed a cement block to the carriage and tied four or five empty beer cans to the block. He wrapped a baby blanket loosely around the assemblage, then waited patiently for the usual crowd to gather. While all attention was on the bespeckled cod being hoisted out of the boats, Eben came around the corner at flank speed pushing the baby carriage before him, roaring some blasphemy about how his wife had produced one baby too many. They couldn't feed the children they had; how could he possibly feed yet another one?

Before the astonished faces of the tourists, he launched the carriage over the pier's edge and into the harbor. It made a mighty splash, and with that cement block as ballast, sank like a stone. All that remained on the surface was a pitiful, hem-torn baby blanket slowly bobbing away on the tide like the wraith of the child it had apparently warmed. As the beer cans slowly exchanged air for water, an artful stream of bubbles came, as if beseechingly, to the surface to be carried gently downtide by the slow-moving current.

Eben stood on the caplog, hands on hips, watching the stream of bubbles swirl and then fade away. He acknowledged the open-mouthed, horror-stricken looks of the audience with a small bow and ducked around the corner to hide in one of the offices, leaving behind all the commotion he could possibly have wished. People ran around bumping into each other. There were some very satisfactory screams, fingers pointing to the bobbing blue blanket, and calls for the police.

But the dock workers barely looked up as they went on with their tasks. They were used to Eben's antics. They had fish to box and trucks to load. When asked for help, one of the workers calmed the swelling tempest with, "Don't mind Eben. He's just bored."

Only the fact that these men stoically went about their accustomed tasks prevented the occasion from becoming a full-scale riot.

It wasn't too long after that episode that the present day observation deck was built for the tourists.

***

Fishermen can make mistakes, some of them too delightful to ignore. Ed, a longtime commercial fisherman, was a man very sure of himself and his place on this planet. He was also one of the best fishermen in the fleet. The income of commercial fishermen fluctuates a great deal over the year. During the stormy winter weather they can rarely leave the harbor and their income wanes. Consequently Ed, like all of his kind, went fishing at every opportunity in the calmer months of the year. Fishing didn't stop because the weekends rolled around. If the weather was good, you went out.

Ed's wife eventually took umbrage at this fact. She wanted at least one day a month when the family could get together during the Cape's delightful summer weather.

Ed picked a warm and windless Sunday, loaded the paraphernalia for a summer's day at the beach into their skiff, and went to the shoals and flats on the west side of Monomoy. With the dropping tide there were plenty of flats for the kids to run around on and there was no way they could hurt themselves. The thought also occurred to Ed that when the tide was at its lowest it would be possible to dig a mess of Hospital Creek clams (some of the world's best) for dinner.

Ed gave in to the soft summer breezes, the warm sun, and his picnic laden stomach. It was time for a little snooze. About the time he was drifting off, his five-year-old came running over, all excited.

"Dad, Dad, come quick, there's a big fish stuck in one of the tide pools!"

Ed raised himself on one elbow and looked over to where little Del was pointing. Sure enough, some distance away, there was a good-sized, gray bodied fish thrashing around, trapped in a shallow tidal pool. Ed had seen all the sharks he ever wanted to; indeed he regarded them as competitors for the fish he caught. He wasn't about to be bothered by watching one of them expire in a tide pool.

"Del, relax. It's just a shark. Look at it all you want, but stay away from it, and don't bother me for awhile."

When Ed woke from his nap, he looked around for his family. They and another family who had just arrived were gathered at the tidal pool around the still-thrashing shark. Ed grunted, rolled to his feet, and headed down the beach, savoring the peace and tranquillity of Monomoy's west side—that is, until he joined his wife and children and saw the cause of the little gathering on the sands.

The "shark" was, in fact, a twelve-foot, six-inch swordfish, one of the most valuable fish in the ocean. The other family had a rope on it, and by rights, it was theirs. It was six inches longer than their skiff; they had to tow it back with the bill tied over the transom.

They were paid a princely sum for this great creature. An article in the paper quoted the tourist as gleefully saying the swordfish paid for his entire vacation.

Poor Ed. He who brooked no nonsense, he who had winter bills as yet unpaid, was in a terrible fix. He had let a very valuable prize literally slip through his fingers and he knew he would surely be kidded about it for the rest of his life. He was right. The episode provided fisherman with chuckles for years and it still provides a chuckle now and then among those who remember.

But in all fairness to Ed, it must be said that the shoal, tepid waters of the inside of Monomoy are about the last place one would expect to see such an oceanic fish, about akin to seeing wild camels roaming the main street of Chatham.

Ed, though, still doesn't see much humor in the fact that he, an experienced fisherman, had let a valuable swordfish go. He quit the commercial fishing business not long after that episode on the sands.

Part II
Monomoy Antics

The Cape Codder Newspaper

The salt water that surrounds this peninsula is and has always been the Cape's linchpin. The fish-laden sea, the shellfish-laden shoals, and even the soggy borders of this sea-girt land have provided sustenance during all the centuries humans have occupied this land. Early on, when our lives were closer to the good earth, even salt hay was an article of commerce. In an August 15, 1946, edition of *The Cape Codder*, Fred Pierce of East Orleans recounted memories of salt haying:

> Some of the older people will well remember the stacks [of hay] along the West Barnstable and Sandwich marshes, stacked two or three feet above the edge of the marshes so the tide might go under them without wetting them or washing them away... I remember as a boy looking out of the train windows for those stacks when passing by.
>
> On the marshes from our present parking ground at Orleans Beach down to the Orleans Coast Guard station and below, the farmers used mowing machines and horse rakes, and gathered it quite quickly and without too much trouble. Occasionally a horse got in a slough hole, but on the whole it was quite easily landed in the fields near the barns.
>
> Years ago Capt. M. M. Pierce, keeper of the Orleans Station told me that he had seen the footprints of oxen on the marshes very distinctly after a severe storm had washed away parts of the sand dunes very suddenly showing the ox tracks quite clearly before the sand would be blown back covering them, showing that many years ago oxen were used instead of horses.

Over on the Tonset Shore other methods were used. There were several scows twenty feet long, broad and shallow draught, which would carry a mowing machine and several men aboard, the old white horse swimming at the stern, across the narrow part of the channel to the marshes beyond.

Previous to this all mowing was done by hand, but last along by machine and scowed across to the Tonset Shore, mostly by the Snows…

Freeman Snow… was noted for being able to put an extra keen edge on his scythe and tools, thus mowing more easily than some, while Uncle Clement never could get an edge on his scythe, thus mowing by force of strength. The men wanted to see what would happen if Uncle Clement had a sharp edge on his scythe for once, so after much persuasion they got his scythe and turned the grindstone for Uncle Freeman to put on an extra keen edge, which required much grinding, and then returned it to Uncle Clement. They had an understanding among themselves to glance over their shoulders to watch Uncle Clement, who forgot himself and put the same amount of effort in his stoke as usual the next morning, which caused him to spin around several times before he could stop and say, "I promise you I cannot use any such a scythe as that."

Shortly after this no salt hay was cut, but only fresh hay and now almost none of that. The oxen, the horses, the scows and the haying of salt hay in these parts are forgotten and a thing of the past."

This salt hay was gathered as animal feed and bedding. It wasn't by any means the best, but it was free and plentiful, strong inducements for its use by thrifty Cape Codders.

But not all Cape Codders were totally involved in the practical aspects of life. The earliest peoples made time for the beauty that surrounds us. In 1948 my great-aunt, Geneva Eldredge, was interviewed by *The Cape Codder* on the subject of "Mayflowering":

Long ago when only the Indians lived on Cape Cod, there grew on the edges of sunny banks and around the trees where the sunbeams played, the daintiest, sweetest little pink and white flowers that filled the air with fragrance.

The copper-colored Indian maidens picked them as they wandered through the woodland paths, and tucked them in their long black braids, saying to each other, "Winter has gone and spring is here again." And the old squaws outside the wigwams, wrapped in their blankets of deer and wolf skins, welcomed the sight of the little flowers and rejoiced that spring had come at long last to drive away the chill of winter.

Years went by and in April of 1637 the first Cape Cod pioneers came riding down the Indian trails to make a settlement in what is now known as Sandwich. Ten stalwart men on horseback, their wives with babies in their arms, riding on pillions behind the saddles that held their husbands. Each man looked ahead as he followed the winding trail over hill and hollow, and thought of the farms and homes they would build in this new land to which they were going.

The women, glancing down the pine needle-littered trail, glimpsed the little patches of pink and white flowers the women in Plymouth called 'Mayflowers.'

And as they sniffed the fragrance, they felt it must be a goodly land where they would make their new homes, if such beauty and sweetness grew wild in the woodlands.

And so the years have gone and still in 1948 the pink and white blossoms of the mayflower are just as sweet and fragrant as when the Indian maidens picked them in the long dim past, and rejoiced at their promise of spring.

We still rejoice at spring's handmaidens, the mayflowers, and the seasonal change they presage.

Another of the articles was about a man I knew who commuted to Monomoy, that spectacularly beautiful island just south of Chatham. He usually traveled by beach buggy, occasionally by plane.

Winnie, who was at least two generations older than I, was a wonderful man. You always had the feeling a chuckle was close at hand when Winnie was around. And it was. "The Shanty," referred to in this June 10, 1948 article titled, "Winnie Bearse Age 70, Flies to his Paradise at Monomoy Point," was just a short distance from our own shanty and most weekends, particularly in the winter, these were the only two camps that were occupied.

Many younger men would hesitate to jump into a light airplane and fly eight miles out on the lonely sands of Monomoy Point to spend a weekend or a week.

But not Winfield M. Bearse, age 70, of Chatham. For several years now he has been flying to his favorite haunt far from the jangle of telephone bells, the carbon monoxide of the streets and the threats of war and violence to pursue his favorite sports.

In the fall and winter he takes his shotgun out to the Point to hunt for gamebirds which abound there, and to catch and cook the shellfish there. In the summer when his friends go out to cast for salt water gamefish, Winnie goes along because he says, there's no place in the world quite as real and rustic as Inward Point, just eight miles out of Chatham on Monomoy Point.

Hardly a month of the year passes that Winnie doesn't hire a Piper Cub plane and a pilot to ferry out to "The Shanty," a small home by the sea at Inward Point where shellfish thrive in the flats, fish are numerous in the water and, in season, the wildfowl fill the skies.

Some months ago Winnie and three of his cronies, Joshua Eldredge, 86, Ernest Eldredge, 72, and Bill Eldredge, 72 ventured out to The Shanty by plane to spend a pleasant weekend hunting and fishing.

"I was the baby of the lot," noted Winnie. The combined ages of the quartet totaled three centuries of Cape Cod longevity.

Winnie Bearse has been going to Monomoy Point for more than a half a century. A carpenter, he first went out as a youth of 17 to help repair the Coast Guard stations and to move them inward, away from the grip of the ever restless tidewaters constantly washing away the sand and threatening at any time to undermine the foundations.

That is when Winnie acquainted himself with the wonders of Monomoy Point which, to so many, is considered a barren spit of land. Winnie and his friends see in the Point a paradise of plenty. Plenty of fish in the water and edible gamebirds overhead.

When Winnie first went to Inward Point there were fully 30 shacks there occupied in the summer by fishermen and their wives and families. At one time the place was so thickly populated that a school was opened for the fishermen's children.

The men went out fishing every day, landing their catches at StageHarbor. The womenfolk helped keep the fishing gear in repair, cared for the children and the shanties and cooked the meals. When cold weather came they moved back to the mainland but they were always ready for the trip back to Inward Point when the spring fish run opened.

In those days the men carried their families and equipment out to the Point on horse-drawn barges having wheels with wide tires so they wouldn't sink into the sand. Later came automobiles with oversized tires, and outboard motor boats. But now many of those seeking the quiet life of Monomoy Point travel by aircraft which land and take off readily on the sand.

A hunting enthusiast, Winnie cares little for sportfishing. But he is always ready to go along with a party of fishermen for a day or a week or even longer.

Often Winnie goes out a day before the others to tidy up The Shanty, gather in a harvest of shellfish and prepare a potful of quahog chowder or oyster stew.

"There's plenty of quahogs out there and some oysters," he said. "A few years ago the scallops were so thick that you couldn't walk through the eel grass without walking on them. When the eel grass disappeared the scallops went too, but the eel grass is coming back now.

"One night I went down by plane ahead of the others who were coming next morning. When I woke up in the morning the wind was blowing hard and the Bay was filled with white water. The weather was so bad I knew the others couldn't come.

"Before I left, I told the others if they couldn't come to send the aviator down to get me anytime he wanted to. Late in the afternoon I was frying a spider full of oysters for my supper when I thought I heard a plane.

"I went out and there was a plane circling over the shanty. I signaled for him to land and he lit. I gave the aviator all of the quahogs I had planned to use for chowder for the others and told him to come back and get me later, maybe tomorrow.

"Earl Allen, one of the owners of The Shanty, had sent the plane out for me because he thought I might be out of kerosene. But I had plenty. When you are down to the beach you have to fo'lay. I had plenty of coffee, canned beans, canned chicken, spaghetti, butter and shellfish. I couldn't leave those fried oysters."

Winnie likes to tell of the cargo of Belgium alcohol, 194 proof, he says, that came ashore at Monomoy during prohibition… Belgium alcohol was so plentiful at the time it was used for fuel to singe the ducks shot there.

"There's still plenty of that Belgium alcohol in town today," he said. "It came in with the tide in five gallon cans. The authorities came down to take it over but by the time they got here it was all out of sight."

Despite the chill wind and storms that dominate Monomoy Point, The Shanty is always a comfortable haven… Its large kitchen range fueled by driftwood provides sufficient heat on the coldest nights. A gasoline mantle lamp illuminates the kitchen and sends its rays through the windows and far out to sea. The gang usually plays cards before retiring. A hand pump with a pipe only a few feet in the sand provides sweet water until an occasional over-sized tide mixes salt water with the fresh to give the campers a taste of brackish water.

A gunning companion of Vernon Eldredge, Winnie finds the marshes and inlets near Inward Point a "hunters" paradise. The two men make frequent trips to the Point during the winter, shooting geese and ducks aplenty for their own use and for an occasional handout to friends.

"We catch plenty for our own use and cook it right at The Shanty, but we never shot more than we needed," he said. "When the tide is out, the fowl travel far out on the flats to eat. When the tide comes in, it drives the birds in and that's when the gunning is good. There used to be a lot of brant out there but you seldom see them now."

Few trees exist in the neighborhood of Inward Point but there is a large huckleberry swamp and a prosperous cranberry bog there, according to Winnie. Ditches through the bog indicate it was once cultivated. However, the bog has grown wild for many years. It still produces a good crop. Men who go down hunting in the fall often bring back a barrel or more of cranberries.

Before he traveled to the Point in a plane, Winnie sometimes used to go out in an outboard motor boat with Earl Allen. The trip took an hour from Stage Harbor.

Despite the efforts of his friends to get him interested in sport fishing, Winnie still is cool to that sport.

Sometimes Vernon would hook a fish and say, Here Winnie, haul him in while I light my pipe." Those were about the only times I ever caught any. I'd rather go quahoging. They were so big, 12 quahogs would open a dry quart.

Winnie's friends had to talk fast to get him to make his first airplane trip "down to the beach" at Inward Point. But after that he needed no coaxing.

He was born in Chatham, the son of Martin Bearse, and has been a carpenter "all his days."

Comeuppance

Monomoy is a barrier beach of sorts, though there is no land mass behind it. Mostly it is the ocean's sweepings from the rest of the Cape.

The always eroding ocean never stops moving the sand flank of the Outer Cape. A small fraction resurfaces to become this sparkling white island which became a playground for my generation.

Driving on this beach or any other is somewhat like messing around in boats, fun and occasionally educational. But the fun is always tempered with a slight degree of challenge. Not every beach trip proceeds just as scheduled. Sooner or later the beach humbles all who drive it. A prosperous cousin, Jake, was showing my father and me his spanking new, very expensive, four-wheel-drive Jeep, the very first of the Wagoneers. The demonstration was conducted on North Beach, a ten-mile long barrier beach that protects much of Chatham from the Atlantic. The new car drove beautifully, smooth as silk. Its virtues were endless. This was the best beach vehicle ever built, or so he would have us believe. And grudgingly, we had to admit this car was a vast improvement over the old two-wheel-drive clunkers we were used to.

"This car will go anywhere," Jake bragged. "It'll take a lot to stick this one."

Cousin was becoming increasingly imperious on the matter of his new beach car, and we still had about five miles of beach driving to go. The worst part of his litany was the fact that he was right. It was superior to anything yet devised, and it did go beautifully. If only there was some way to stop the endless praises.

It turned out that we didn't have to think of a way to stop those paeans of praise—a little snow and windblown sand took care of that task quite nicely.

Snowstorms on the beach can be beautiful things. The near constant winds swirl and curl the snow in sinuous shapes around the dunes. Free form, free-flowing wind sculptures are snow shadows of the dunes themselves. An earlier February snowstorm brought beauty to our eyes and comeuppance to our driver at the same time. The snows came, the wind howled, and then the snow stopped and the wind kept blowing, covering the newly drifted snow with a patina of sand. More than a patina in some places. Cousin, majestically wheeling the (by now) sickeningly agile new vehicle through the dunes, drove unsuspectingly out on one of these sand-covered snow drifts—drove so fast that the entire car was suspended on two feet of sandy snow.

The scenario: driving along at twenty miles an hour, listening to the monotonous accounts of this car's many virtues; then WHOOMP, all four wheels were two feet-off the ground suspended on snow, with no hope of moving. The agile new car was now about as agile as an aground boat.

This was not a good situation. We were hopelessly stuck, five miles from the nearest help, in bitter cold, and with no tools of any sort with which to extricate ourselves.

"Well Jake, unless you can teach this thing to levitate it looks like *we've* got ourselves a problem."

Cousin Jake just grunted. What had to be done was to remove most of the sand/snow mix from under the car in order to lower the car back down to the beach to let the tires get some purchase on the beachsand—or wait for spring.

Both of the adults on this expedition were on the far edge of overweight and lightly dressed. The youngest member of the group, myself, was lithe, dressed for winter, gullible, and expendable. The gullible one went under the two-ton car with the still hot exhaust system and excavated volumes of snow mixed with sand—a mixture I soon came to loathe. And all I had to work with were just gloved hands and a board we found on the wrackline. An added fillip to this most disagreeable job was the occasional dropping of the car as the snow supports were dug out from under it. I had quickly learned to avoid the hot exhaust pipes, but it was hard to avoid the whole car inching down over me. On the other hand, this incremental squeezing sharpened my digging instincts wonderfully. When enough material had been dug out and seconds before terminal congealing set in, I was extricated and the Wagoneer was started. After a few false starts, the Jeep pulled itself out of this most peculiar situation. There wasn't a whole lot said about the virtues of the vehicle on the ride home, and as I remember it, we were never again invited for a ride in that wonderful beach car.

Monomoy loomed on the horizon of my life like a distant galaxy, bright, distant, and beckoning. The lure of the island was all but irresistible. When it became legal for me to drive, most of my energies revolved around the pristine sands of that beautiful peninsula.

Monomoy was, and is, a goal I also equate with happiness. And I don't know why. Certainly all my experiences on the island have not been happy. Indeed, some of my major adolescent agonizings were worked out on the island. But somehow, for some reason, Monomoy has always equaled pure pleasure in my memory banks. Monomoy no longer has a working lighthouse, but for me there will always be a bright, shining light over that island.

But this section of the book is about humbling experiences and the following occurred on the island that has captivated my soul for most of my life.

My close friend, Jimmy, and I had just such a learning experience in the Chatham cut-through one cold winter's day. In Cape Cod parlance, a cut-through is where the ocean cuts through a land mass. In this instance it was where the constantly eroding ocean had finally broken through a narrowing strand of sand into the tranquil waters of Stage Harbor and made Monomoy an island. It was a moat we were to cross many times in forthcoming years.

Again, like so many of our experiences, we had not thought through the trip we were to make. We just assumed we would make it, and we were partly right. We were also partly wrong. Oh, how cruelly wrong!

On a late winter trip to Monomoy, we rowed across the cut-through by Horne's Cottages in our dried-out wooden skiff.

Wood swells and shrinks as it absorbs or loses moisture. Therefore, a wooden boat left out of water for any length of time will leak lustily for a day or two until the wood swells and the seams shut. The skiff we used had been sitting overturned on the bank all fall and most of the winter. It was porous.

We had gathered the necessary gear for a weekend at the camp (mostly food) and set out across the cut-through in the seam-spurting rowboat. In our haste we forgot to bring a bailer but decided we probably wouldn't need one, since it was only a couple of hundred feet across the cut. It became quite obvious halfway across the channel that the boat was sinking faster than we were rowing; it became obvious that it was going to be a close thing. We had to keep rowing, but as the boat sank deeper and deeper it went slower and slower, and as it went slower, it filled faster. As the boat filled, a very shaky balancing act ensued. We reverted to paddling, one of us at each end of the boat, to more evenly distribute our weight, and at that, we barely made it. As the sinking boat went out from under us, the only thing we weren't able to grab was the wax paper bundle on the stern seat. I can still see that lovingly wrapped, package, a still-warm, homemade, frosted chocolate cake, bobbing at the whim of the wind, bobbing away from us, curtsying out of reach—a frosted chocolate cake! Leaking boats were a fact of life, but this was the first time I realized that leaking boats could also be cruel as well as sink.

Today's fiberglass boats do away with all thoughts of early spring sinkings. Today we could take that chocolate cake across the harbor and down to the camp without a thought (if we didn't eat it en route). I don't miss those leaky skiffs, but they did lend a bit of excitement and daring to any trip as to whether the boat, and you, would make it or sink. How fast those soggy spring rituals and trials have gone from our lives. How quickly they have been forgotten. It's as if they never were. Thank you technology. Come to think of it, if we had eaten that frosted chocolate cake, we would quickly have forgotten all about it, no matter how good it tasted. By its floating away (no quick sinking, just a slow fading out of sight in the dusk as it bobbed away on the offshore breeze), we can still hunger for it. Not bad. Still hungering for a fifty-year-old cake. I'm kind of glad now it floated away. I sometimes wonder where that cake washed up and if someone found and appreciated it. The good ship

"Chocolate Cake" was bound north for Pleasant Bay when last seen. With a fair wind and fair tide, she should have made landfall in South Orleans about eight o'clock that evening, ready for a hungry early morning beach walker. I wonder if foxes like chocolate cake?

The camp we were headed for was a five-mile walk down the bleak, late winter beach. With the north wind pushing us along, the trek was in no way onerous. Long to be sure, a bit of a challenge, but fun.

It has just occurred to me as I write this, that for nearly all of the folks in Chatham, Monomoy was by no means a popular place. It was close to town, yet there were rarely more than half a dozen of us on the island at any one time. Far more often we were the only inhabitants.

Once Monomoy became an island, what little traffic there had been all but ceased. Reliable, affordable outboards were somewhere in the future, as were reliable cars. Four-wheel-drive cars were way out of reach. There really wasn't much point in barging a car across if you didn't have a camp on the island. All the mainland beaches were uncrowded and equally pristine. What was the sense of struggling to get to an island, when the same waters and the same uncrowded beaches could be sampled just a short drive down any road?

But having a camp, however mean, meant having a base, a focus, something to work on and to improve. It provided a reason to have a car on the beach. And at least for this teenager, it was something to cling to. Monomoy meant more, far more, than just a thin strip of white sand crowned with waving, emerald-green, verdant grasses.

My folks, inveterate Monomoy lovers, had taken me to the island at the earliest possible opportunity. And except for some wartime restrictions I've been going there ever since. As some youngsters use sports to alleviate the very real agonies of adolescence, I used the island for the same purpose and came to love it. Out there were few people to frustrate my learning curve. As an added attraction, there were rarely any audiences for the many times I had to extricate myself from some scrape or other. Facing a certain five- or ten-mile walk through soft beach sand wonderfully sharpened my ability to figure out why the old car wouldn't go and to fix it on the spot. There were many such opportunities, and almost always the decrepit car got us back to the harbor's edge.

The high school years were difficult for me. My grades teetered on the edge of disaster. Somehow, I had figured out how to stay just ahead of failure by doing the bare minimum of schoolwork and there I stayed. But on Monomoy that didn't matter. In Monomoy's classroom I was an apt student.

At age fifteen, I was six feet, four inches tall and about an inch in diameter. There wasn't a door frame I didn't whack or a threshold I didn't trip over. It seemed as if my brain was often computing my height at three inches less than reality. Indeed, once while courting a girl, I was invited to meet her parents. Thinking to make a good impression, I knocked at the front door of their 200-year-old dwelling. The solemn father ushered me from the tiny foyer into the living room, where the assembled family was waiting to inspect the latest of the circling males. I wanted to make a good impression, so I strode right in—and hit my head so hard on the door frame I was driven to my knees before them all. I staggered to a couch and tried to pass it off as just a slight bump, even though I was having trouble seeing straight. It hurt so much that an involuntary tear oozed out of one eye and at about the same time, I also felt a warm trickle of blood coursing down my scalp. I surreptitiously wiped away the lachrymose liquid and tilted my head back in the forlorn hope that maybe no one would notice the bleeding. A pony-sized Newfoundland dog ambled amiably in and plopped his huge head on my leg, just asking for a friendly pat or two. Thinking to redeem myself and still seeing with swimming eyes, I gave the dog a hearty pat on the hindquarters. The animal collapsed with a groan at my feet (it was sixteen years old). With my awash eyes I hadn't noticed the gray around the muzzle. The robust pat had knocked the poor dog's hindquarters out from under him. I had made my impression.

All during high school, awkwardness was my middle name. I was not particularly sports minded; I was much too ungainly to coordinate any action. Monomoy's sweeping sand dunes and clam-littered flats offered little to collide with; it was a place where I felt comfortable.

I lived in the remotest part of town, five miles west of Main Street. I was the only one from that part of town in my class (twenty-three in total). I felt not quite shunned but really not part of the townies either. Monomoy became my town and I felt quite at home there.

Was it lonely out on the outskirts of town? I suppose it was—just as it was lonely on Monomoy. But I never felt lonely; there was always plenty to do. Something always needed fixing; there were clams to dig, fish to catch, and always on Cape Cod's campus something to learn more about.

Alcohol never played any part in our doings on the island. We were known then and now as the non-drinking Eldridges. We didn't have anything against drinking. We just didn't need it to have side-splitting times and come to think of it, we had little or no money left over for alcohol; we could barely afford the gasoline.

A few others on the island made up for our lack in that department, but never in any destructive way. Earl Allen's shanty over on a nearby dune was used about as often as ours, and nearly every weekend there was a gang there and some quiet drinking. There wasn't a soul around except us and they never bothered anyone.

On one occasion though, one of them made the elementary mistake of going south when they were driving off the beach. The fog of fermented grain was too thick for them to notice that the ocean was on the wrong side for the trip they were taking. All went well for about five miles or so, until the beach ended. Not deterred in the slightest, they resolutely continued on a southerly course, straight for Nantucket's Great Point eleven miles distant. Unfortunately, the beach curved around to the west.

When the icy waters of the North Atlantic came up around their knees, the alcohol haze dissipated somewhat. The men waded out of the surf, up onto the beach and wondered where they might be. They certainly weren't at Stage Harbor, their destination. About the time they were beginning to realize the enormity of their mistake, we drove up, saw the half-submerged car and the two confused and surprisingly sanguine men, and realized what had happened. We towed the car out of the surf up onto high beach and took Earl and Winnie back to the harbor's edge. We knew them well for the kindly men they were. They had often offered us kids leftover apple pies or a platter of cookies that hadn't been consumed by their gang. It was good to be able to return their kindness.

But Monomoy wasn't the only place where the haze of alcohol played havoc. The Outer Cape is noted for its abundance of fog. A few belts of rum and a bit of fog are all the ingredients needed for confusion to exist.

In his delightful little treatise, "The Bay as I See It," my grandfather Nickerson tells the story about Uncle Miah and Uncle Tull. In those days, around the turn of the century, oldsters in the communities were called *Uncle This* or *Aunt That*. Tull and Miah were two well-known salt haymakers who were working the marshes of Pleasant Bay and found a little fog:

> They sculled around in the flat calm until their two jugs of rum were used up, and finally ran their scow into what looked like a bed of live eel-grass growing on the shore.
>
> "You set still Miah, I'll jump out and pull the boat ashore."
>
> With that, over the bow he went and plumb down out of sight through the eel-grass, which proved to be just a loose patch drifting aimlessly about, as so often happens.
>
> Uncle Miah managed somehow to get the dazed and half-drowned Uncle Tull back aboard the scow again; and by now the fog had thinned somewhat so they thought they could make out the land. But their rum haze was at its thickest; and they both swore they had never seen this coast before, unless it was the coast of Labrador with which they were both familiar. They worked the boat ashore and, hat in hand, Uncle Tull made his wavering way up the path to a house they had discovered in the trees. He knocked gingerly, and when the door opened enough so he could see a buxom woman through the crack, he queried apologetically, "Good woman, can you tell me who lives here?"
>
> The answer came like a bolt of chain lightening and nearly knocked the unsteady Uncle Tull off his feet.
>
> "Sure I can tell you who lives here. And I'll tell that drunken, good for nothing, husband of mine down there in the boat, too, if he ever gets sobered up enough to walk up the hill to his own door."

But alcohol wasn't our problem. Learning the many lessons in the process of growing up took all our time and most of our energies.

Figuring out the intricacies of getting together with the other half of the human race, girls, was a major instructional gap, one that occupied more and more of our thoughts. There were no guide books, no way to bridge the gap except by wading in and testing. It was much like learning where the dangers lay in the shoals and riptides of our local waters: we just had to experiment. And like our watery education this new learning was fraught with anxiety and sleepless nights.

The immediate postwar years, at least for a lot of us, were a time of innocence, both in world affairs and in getting together with the opposite sex. We were both ignorant and innocent but we were eagerly trying to learn the ways of the world. Like most kids of our ilk and times, we stumbled and fumbled our way through the uncharted waters of closeness. And as with learning the waters around Cape Cod, we ran aground many times, only to get out of the shallow waters and try again. We were learning where those hazards were, and we wouldn't make the same mistake again.

Looking back on our actions, I'm amazed we were ever able to get any girl to go out with us more than once, though once was enough for most of them.

One of our pitiful attempts to get close to girls involved black fog and the Stonehorse Lightship, located just a quarter of a mile off Monomoy's southeast shore.

Fog is a fact of life on the Outer Cape. The season between winter and the too-short summer is a time of atmospheric unrest as the cold ocean slowly warms. Fog is most common in the spring, and that silent fog is a ventriloquist.

We used the fog to some small advantage. When we took a new date down the beach in the black fog, we would often park as close as possible to the invisible lightship. We knew where it was by the flotsam on the beach. Our date had no idea a lightship was close at hand. Once the unmuffled, roaring car motor was quelled, all that would be heard for a few seconds would be the murmur of the sibilant waves. Then, out of that gray opaque wall, would come the blasting, blatting, ear-splitting, windshield-rattling sound of that powerful fog horn. It was usually enough to bring the new date scurrying across the seat.

Another one of our maneuvers was to go to Hardings Beach in West Chatham on any summer beach day. There were always girls arrayed along the warm sands. It was just a matter of selecting a bunch that looked likely and talking up the wonders of the Cape. The talk would be steered around to the glimmering island plainly visible across the blue waters. Monomoy, from Hardings Beach, always looked as though it had a halo over it. The sun reflecting off those bright sands and the ever-present salt spray made the air above the island glow. A most enticing sight.

The next step would be to let it be known, subtly of course, that we had a car on the island, that we would be happy to take the girls for a ride on those inviting sands, and that not seeing Monomoy while they had the opportunity was little short of dereliction of duty while visiting the Cape.

The girls usually felt safety in their numbers. Our scheme was to take them all for a short spin in the beach car, then after a selection process, winnow out a likely one from the herd for a solo and longer trip down the beach.

It was a grand scheme for optimistic teenagers, but things didn't always go as planned.

One gorgeous summer day my friend, Jim Eldredge, gathered three or four likely beauties from a stellar crop at Hardings Beach. They agreed to meet at Stage Harbor for the promised trip over the sands. The four girls apparently felt that their numbers needed reinforcements, so they brought along two of their friends. They didn't realize that Jim was more or less harmless. Now, there were six girls and Jim, more than a boatload. Two rowing trips would take too long, so Jim decided to take a chance, to try to take them all across the harbor at once. And all went well—for awhile.

Boats stay afloat when they have ample freeboard, ample enough to ride over any waves that they encounter. Freeboard is the distance from the waterline to the edge, or the gunwale, of the boat. As the freeboard decreases, the ability to ride over the waves also decreases. Water sloshes in, the freeboard decreases, more water surges in, and the occupants are swimming. It's pretty straightforward.

Jim knew he had a problem. The freeboard was all of two inches when eight inches would have been marginal, but he thought he could make it; the harbor was calm. The girls had no idea how perilous their situation was. At the midpoint of the tranquil harbor crossing, a deep-draft trap boat thundered by, dragging a monstrous wake—a wake that was sure to swamp the overloaded skiff. Jim endeared himself to all those girls in a flash. Seeing what was coming and knowing the outcome, he handed his wallet to the most comely gal and immediately jumped overboard. Without his weight aboard, the little skiff stayed afloat as it rode sluggishly over the waves. Jim stayed overboard and swam the boat to the island. All hands were safe and dry and Jim's reputation was greatly enhanced.

As a postscript to this little tale, Jim's quick thinking and even quicker selection was rewarded when he later married the keeper of the wallet.

I hadn't thought of this before, but those times on the beach really were a selection process for both sexes. Girls that couldn't tolerate our manic moves never came back. The few girls that could see beyond our seemingly bizarre antics came back again and again. But there weren't many.

Ed once invited a girl to sample Monomoy's splendor. They rowed across the harbor in the late afternoon, a time when the colors were at their richest. The trip down the beach was uneventful. Ed showed off the beach in the rich light of the setting sun; he also managed to do a little fishing along one of the eastside bars and a little hand-in-hand walking on the deserted beach. As darkness stole the light, they headed off the beach. The tide had come in so far that they were no longer able to drive along the base of the cliff to the usual parking place by the old Coast Guard boathouse. This was no real problem; it happened on every high-course tide. At the most it was a minor inconvenience for all of us that used that parking area.

Living in one of nature's paradises can be limiting to one's understanding of people who haven't been so blessed, and vice versa. Ed's understanding of others grew exponentially that dark night.

He parked the car where it would stay out of the water, and he and his date proceeded to wade the 200 yards back to the skiff by the boathouse. His date had never been in such a situation before, wading in warm, black water with a young man she had just met, and not at all familiar with the creatures underfoot. This same situation was old hat to us devotees of the beach. We knew there was nothing harmful lurking in those dark waters. It was a cloudy night, black dark, one of those unusual nights when visibility was limited to a very few feet. On most normal dark nights it's possible to see some distance despite the darkness. Not this night.

The neophyte to the beach stubbed her toe on the first horseshoe crab that was enjoying the newly submerged sand. Ed told us later her paralyzing scream could have been the cause for cardiac arrest for anyone within hearing distance, anyone in Chatham. Ed had no idea what was the matter. Horseshoe crabs were a fact of life in the warm waters of the Cape. Something not worth commenting on.

There was a second scream, as yet another all but blind horseshoe crab (these ancient animals are up to a foot across and utterly harmless) blundered into her feet. Ed's date fled back to the old car, vowing never to go in that black water ever again.

It was at least three hours until the tide would drop enough to allow dry land access to the skiff. Ed had to go to work the next day; he wasn't about to wait out the tide. No amount of reasoning did the slightest bit of good. That girl refused to set foot in the creature-filled water.

Ed offered to piggyback the frightened girl back to the waiting skiff. No dice. This neophyte wasn't about to go piggybacking with strange men. Ed offered to fetch the skiff and bring it to her. Nothing doing. This girl had no intention of waiting alone in the dark.

Ed, the most gentle of men, was close to the limit of his patience. He told us later that only the threat of leaving her alone on the island goaded her into action. Faced with the choice of braving the harmless horseshoe crabs, being left on the island, or carried back to the skiff, she, after much cajoling, opted for the piggyback transport. Ed never saw this girl again.

I had a few setbacks in this line myself. One attractive new date was supposed to be home by ten o'clock, not one minute later. That was no problem. It was easy to *promise* an early return. We headed down the beach as the sun was setting, a beautiful time to see any natural wonder, a magnificent time to view Monomoy. We took the usual route, down by the sweeping dunes on the outside road to the tip of the beach, the threshold of Point Rip, that riotous stretch of turbulent white water reaching toward Nantucket just over the horizon. Then it was back through the dunes for a look at a family of foxes living under the collapsed Middle Station barn. We watched the antics of those beguiling little creatures until it became too dark to see. Few animals are as cute in action or looks as fox cubs.

The last bit of Monomoy I wanted to show my date was the family camp at Inward Point. We were already pushing the ten o'clock curfew somewhat, but the visit to the camp would only take a few minutes. It wasn't far out of the way.

It was a still night and the old car didn't have any headlights. Few of our cars did. We rarely needed them; most night skies gave enough light for us to see our way. There were rarely any other cars on the beach, so the dangers of limited visibility was minimal. Most of the time.

On this night an unusually high tide had flooded the road into the camps. The windless night combined with the darkness gave no hint that three feet of water covered the normally dry road. I drove onto the road with total unawareness. There was an almighty splash, and when we got ourselves sorted out, the water was up over the seats, the floorboards floating in our laps. Any hopes of meeting the ten o'clock deadline sank with the waterlogged car. It was a soggy, silent, five-mile walk off that beach, five miles in soft beach sand toward an irate and worried father awaiting our return.

As with Ed's experience, the girl vanished, never again to feel Monomoy's warm embrace, or mine.

Low beach driving was something we all did. The hard-packed sand between the tide lines gave us a chance to go faster than our usual ploddings. Down next to the surf on the wave-packed sand we could cruise along in third gear, something we could never do on high beach. Low beach was the beach of choice for this very reason.

Again we (yet another date and I) were exploring Monomoy's charms. We came across Westy Keene, a good friend and fellow Monomoyite, and his date doing the same. We had both stopped to watch the baby foxes gambol the early evening away. And again, darkness drove us back toward the harbor. It was low tide and that meant an easy ride up the surf line. There were never any problems with low beach driving.

We headed off under the lash of yet another early curfew. As always, the car's lights had long ago gone the way of its fenders, victims of the saltwater we constantly drove in and through. But the softly surging, white surfline gave us an easy guide. All we had to do was stay ten feet or so above it and we would be back in no time. It had been a successful trip, the new date suitably impressed, and the possibilities for future dates looked promising. All was right with the world.

Then, suddenly, out of the darkness there was the briefest glimpse of a dark blur and we became airborne. It was most peculiar. One minute we were chugging along the smooth beach, the next we were heading for the stars with no warning amid a cacophony of rending steel. All that changed when the old car next made contact with the good earth. There was an ear-splitting crash and we were immediately immersed in steam and gas fumes. The old Model A wasn't much of a flyer, but she landed with authority and lurched to a rust-flaking stop.

My date's head had cracked the windshield and I had bent the steering wheel. The car, my pride and joy, was an inert lump of metal, oozing liquids. Luckily, Westy eventually came along. With his car pulling and my date and I pushing, we managed to get my beach-weary "A" up on high beach out of the reach of the oncoming surf. The ride back to the harbor's edge was a silent one. I'm sure that my date was wondering what she was doing on that beach with an apparent maniac. I was wondering if the old car was fixable. No, I wasn't callous. The two of us were obviously fine, dented but functioning. We would heal, but what about my much-loved car?

The old car survived its only flight after a bit of surgery. Two new motor mounts, an oak spliced frame, a new gas line, reconnected radiator hoses, and odds and ends of bent metal were hammered straight to serve again. The windshield was only cracked on the passenger side, no need to replace that. The steering wheel was pried back to a semblance of straightness. In those days it was easy to love an old car. They were inexpensive, easy to fix, and gave you everything they had to give. How could you not love them?

Luck plays a big part in life. No adult would deny that. Most of my life, good luck has been sitting on my shoulder, and I'm so very glad she has chosen to do that. On that beach, on that night, she outdid herself. What had caused the impromptu flight could easily have killed us. Our launching ramp for flight was an enormous stump, waterlogged and slimy, that had chosen that night to deposit itself on low beach in such a manner that the trunk of the defunct tree was facing us. As we came chugging along the beach the bumper slid up over this slippery, inclined trunk and lifted the car up and over the root mass. Had this stump been facing the other way the consequences of our carefree drive would certainly been much more serious. Ah, well.

Ah, Monomoy, moonlight, and memories. For quite a few years Monomoy was but a backdrop for what we thought was our wily pursuit of the fairer sex but what was in reality our clumsy, faltering, but undeviatingly single-minded attempts to form some kind of a bond with those hard-to-understand creatures.

September is when the moon seems so close. The moon was full; it was a perfect night to introduce two fair maidens to the beauty and wonders of Monomoy in the moonlight. We found two such maidens (high school classmates) and headed down to Monomoy's inviting sands. The beach was bathed in a characteristic moon glow of blue white light; the sinuous rutted tracks stretching out in the distance were in a black bas-relief of moon shadow. The fact that the old car had no headlights made no difference at all. We had no trouble at all finding our way to the Point ten miles distant.

We scooped out a shallow pit, filled it with the always available driftwood, and had a nice fire going in no time. Looking east there were no signs of life, just the cloudless sky harboring that enormous moon. To the south we could make out the loom of Nantucket's lights blossoming on the dark horizon. Looking north we could easily see the myriads of twinkling lights that defined the south shore of Cape Cod, all the way from Chatham to Great Island off Hyannis. We could see all around and at the same time were invisible to those we saw. It was a nice cozy feeling.

Watching the sparks from our driftwood fire climbing into the still night sky and seeing the moon's cold golden fire spilling over us made the cooking of hot dogs anti-climatic. We ate the charred offerings with gusto, all the time taking in the beauty of this glorious island. We never realized our talking had little but nuisance value (the girls were nice enough not to let on); the moon and the beach were giving the real message. We were kids—what did we know? I'm also sure there was some fumbled groping that evening; the ingredients were all there—boys, girls, and moonbeams. We would have to have been made of stone not to fall under the influence of that magnificent yellow orb.

But fires, groping, and moonbeams don't stop time. Eventually, as the moon ascended its invisible staircase, we reluctantly had to climb back in the old car to head for home. As always, there were worried fathers to appease. The ride off the beach was of a different mien altogether. The car's occupants were in the snuggling mode, a daunting task in a car with bucket seats separated by the gear shift handle. I had become resigned to a monastic drive up the beach when I realized we had a problem.

That friendly moon that had so nicely put the rutted tracks in such dark relief when it was low on the horizon was by now high in the sky, directly overhead as a matter of fact. Those tracks so obvious early in the evening were now invisible. Everything looked monochromatic, flat, white and beautiful, but where to go? Where were the tracks? We got out of the car and felt around where we thought the tracks might be and eventually found them. We went back to the car, fumbled it into the ruts, and started for home.

Now, one of the good things about a Model A (and there were many) was that if the wheels were in a deep set of ruts, all you had to do was advance the throttle, put the car in first gear, and it would follow the ruts like a bloodhound. We knew that once the car was in the tracks, we'd be home in due time.

But there were two vital things I didn't know. One was that the previous night's easterly had carved away a goodly section of beach, leaving a three- to four-foot sea wall along long stretches of the shore. A sea wall is a vertical wall of beach sand like a giant's step down to the surf. The other vital fact missing from my meager fund of beach knowledge was the all important fact that the tracks we were blissfully following off the beach were not the tracks we had made coming down the beach.

The moon shone unclouded and magnificent, the old car puttered up the tracks, steering itself off the beach, and the occupants were working hard to take advantage of the moon's spell. All was right with our world—until the ruts we were following disappeared into thin air and we very nearly followed them. Two things saved us from a long walk off the beach. One was the fact that the tracks intersected the sea wall at a very shallow angle and the second was that the tide was dropping. The right front wheel dropped into space first, then the right rear tire rather companionably followed the front tire over the sea wall. The car was now at a forty-five degree angle, the right side dangling over the licking surf. That deep left rut was all that prevented the two left wheels (acting as little mushroom anchors) and the car itself from sliding over the minor precipice. It took a few seconds for us to realize what had happened. We were all jammed against the downhill side of the car. The car itself was uneasily teetering on the edge of a four-foot sea wall and the surf was washing the base of that sand wall. Now everything definitely was not right with our world. We were seven miles down the beach in a perched car with the surf six inches from our noses.

We were startled but not hurt. We had been trying to get close to the girls but this was a bit much. We extricated ourselves, crawled out the upper door, and laughingly surveyed the situation. None of us wanted to walk off the beach as long as the car still ran. But right at the moment the only way it looked like it would go was down on its side, in the surf. Luckily the tide was dropping. An incoming tide would have undercut the sea wall even more and the car would have fallen on its side.

Also, fortunately, Model A's were relatively light. The only solution we could see to our predicament was to dig out from under the left front wheel, tug and yank the car around until it was facing the ocean, and push it over the edge. Then, if all went well, we would pile in and drive along between the ocean and the sea wall, until the beach leveled out and we could once again find some ruts that would lead us off the island. Surprisingly, this solution worked, and worked so well that we were on our way in a very short time, leaving the surf victimless but waiting patiently. Jim and I also had to be patient. Once our dates returned home we never saw them again on Monomoy.

Apparently our skills at enticement were proving to be much better than our skills at ensuring a second date. But, like learning the waters of the Cape, we would keep at it and eventually learn our way.

Monomoy, moonlight, and a little moon madness—a perfect recipe for kids. We had tried that recipe and found it delightful, and we would try it again and again. And it still works for older kids, a lot older kids, but kids at heart.

The Ocean's Edge

Monomoy in my lifetime has variously been a peninsula, an island, or as now, in 2000, two islands. This piece of land is the leavings of the glacial till that is the outer arm of Cape Cod. Relentless reshaping takes the sand grains south from the east-facing Wellfleet, Eastham, Orleans, and Chatham beaches. Most of these sand grains serve to shallow the ocean floor; a few of them journey south, far enough to reemerge from the ocean floor, and with the wind as a goad, form the hauntingly beautiful contours of my favorite island. This island is mobile; every bit of it came first by the heavy hand of the glacier and is now being sculpted in its beautiful sinuous forms by the restless winds and surging tides.

Surprisingly this island has some freshwater ponds and some upland vegetation; in fact it is a microcosm of the Cape itself. All of the geological features are constantly changing.

The Shark Hole is halfway down Monomoy's west side, now all but engulfed by sand as a result of the ocean's break at Inward Point.

Five miles southwest of the Shark Hole lies a small, nearly completely sanded-in harbor. It's not navigable now except for creatures of the tidal flats. As geological features go, the harbor is in the last stages of transition from salt water to fresh water and sometime far in the future back to salt water as the ocean reclaims this fragile land.

It wasn't always so. Sometime years ago there was open ocean here. Relentless long-shore tides spurred by buffeting northeast winds gnawed off many cubic yards of the Outer Cape and spewed them south to form a peninsula beach. Every so often this sand buildup was accelerated by stronger than usual climatic forces. This accelerated drift of sand would flow south along the beach, then hook westward and eventually hook around to the north. The result of one of these stronger than usual forces was a delightful little harbor about ten miles out at sea. This two- or three-acre harbor has served man and beast well during its relatively short existence.

Probably the first beneficiaries of this small pond in the ocean were the simplest forms of life, the one-celled creatures, various planktonic life forms, then, moving up the evolutionary ladder, simple seaweeds and sponges able to survive because of the sheltered and warmer waters offered here.

Fishes followed, the small grazers to stay, the larger predators to follow and hopefully catch the small grazers. By the second or third summer of its inception the little pond was a healthy microcosm of plant and animal life. Shellfish covered the surrounding flats, finfish occupied the waters and marine plant life was prevalent in both areas.

This well-established maritime community attracted the attention of Native Americans. The pond offered many different foods in abundance. The prevailing southwest winds held the voracious mosquitoes at bay. What better place to spend the warm months?

The one apparently missing ingredient for human life on this seemingly barren stretch of beach was fresh water. But the natives knew how to find water. They well knew that the fresh rain water percolating through the beach sand will "rest"on the salt water below. Nearly any low spot in the dunes will yield fresh water in abundance just a few inches below the sand. The Native Americans' summer encampments lasted well into the eighteenth century, when the white settlers usurped the area.

Codfish were, even then, becoming hard to find close in along the mainland shores. Boats had to go farther afield to garner reasonable catches. Again, the harbor at sea beckoned. Shanties went up along its shores and men began using it as a harbor of refuge. Soon, the overnight stays became longer. Before long fishermen were spending the season on the shores of this little oasis of calm. It was a protected anchorage and closer to the fishing grounds for these sailing fishermen.

In the late 1800s, a three-master laden with thirteen tons of gunpowder went down in shallow water just a short distance from the little harbor. Salvers were able to salvage a portion of the cargo and for safe-keeping, stored it on the bottom of the pond. Early sulfa-based gun-powders formed a cake or skin when immersed; the interior mass would stay dry for years. At any rate, the harbor acquired a name that prevails to this day, the Powder Hole.

This incident focused more attention on this little harbor at sea. A small seasonal town sprang up on its banks. The shanties were replaced by more substantial buildings and women and children moved down. A school building that doubled as a church on appropriate occasions was subscribed and built. Two substantial piers were built out into Nantucket Sound to accommodate the increasing draft of the larger fishing vessels. Soon, the Powder Hole was a thriving seasonal center of the fishing industry.

The federal government took notice and constructed a very sub-stantial lifesaving station in the midst of the village. Even the state gov-ernment recognized the unique properties of this snug little harbor. They set up a lobster hatchery on the southeasterly side of the Hole.

The advent of reliable gasoline engines heralded the end of man's commercial use of the harbor. The reliability and speed of gasoline-dri-ven fishing boats made the use of this little pond unnecessary for com-mercial purposes. By the 1920s only the lifesaving station was in opera-tion on a regular basis and even it was winding down. The logs reveal a brief flurry of activity during Prohibition days, but otherwise a fast drop in vessel sightings, and therefore a lessening reason for the station's exis-tence. The station was abandoned to the winds of Monomoy in the mid-1940s .

The Powder Hole seemed to adjust its rhythms to that of its users. By the time the Point Station was closed down, the inlet was only nav-igable at high tide and the harbor itself was sanding in. By the time I became interested in this area, in 1946, you could still run an outboard in on the high tides. Small bass, bluefish, and flounder were readily available in season; the flats were covered with delicious, fat clams. These obliging flats were also used as runways by camp owners. Piper Cubs came and went with a fair degree of frequency. All in all, though, the Powder Hole was closing shop. The inlet became increasingly shallow, the sanding in of the main harbor continued unabated, and fewer and fewer people visited the area. No one needed the harbor and the flats became barren as the sips of ocean water lessened.

The ancient anchorage is now a small quarter of an acre of deep water nourished on the extreme high tides by meager infusions of its former nutrients.

A few hundred yards south of the old harbor entrance a new sand hook has recently formed to enclose a small pond. Its flats are teeming with clams. Small bass, bluefish, and an occasional lobster are caught along its shores. Now tourists come in their high-powered boats to visit and exclaim over the beauty of the area.

Shortly after the Second World War the Coast Guard station was deactivated, as mentioned, and was eventually (in the 1960s) demolished in a cataclysmic explosion. The word around Chatham was that this station was to be razed a floor at a time in a series of controlled blasts. Apparently the crew that was dispatched to do the job was too impatient for that scenario. They stuffed the old station with all the explosives they had and touched it off in one grandiose effort. This stoutly built, three-story building that had easily shrugged off the howling winds of Monomoy was no match for the blinding detonation that scattered shattered bits of the structure over two acres of beach. We never found a piece larger than a foot or two, and each of these pieces was so splintered as to be unrecognizable as lumber, save for the many layers of paint applied by often bored Coast Guardsmen during their long tenure on that seemingly bleak beach.

As long as it stood, the white painted building loomed large on the otherwise pristine beach. Never an eyesore, it was always a giant white exclamation point on that otherwise featureless beach, a sturdy reminder of the hazards of the surrounding waters. Two of our close friends had drowned within sight of that station. Point Rip, so beautiful from shore, so attractive to the sport fish, was an unrelenting hazard to men.

Fishing the Surfline

Surf fishing brings on, at least to me, a gentle communion with forces far greater than anything we normally see in life. Those tons of white water sliding up and down the beach require the utmost respect. The sun or moon coming up from the dark ocean turns the vaguely sinister into a friendly seascape. There is magic on the edge of the ocean, and for me, it isn't enough to just stand there and watch it happen. Standing there with a fishpole in hand gives purpose to an otherwise seemingly aimless enjoyment. Fishing is okay, just looking is a bit hedonistic.

My earliest memories of fishing Monomoy were watching my Grandfather Eldridge heave and haul in the roiled waters of the ocean's surf. On arriving at a likely spot, Grampa would rub the drail (a half-pound lead lure with an embedded hook) in the sand to bring out the shine. He would then array a heavy, tarred cotton line along the gently sloping beach in a series of serpentine folds. When all was in readiness, he would whirl that heavy drail over his head like a lariat and release it at the opportune time to sail far out over the water. Then it was just a matter of the hand over hand, refolding the line on the beach for the next try. It was hard work with little finesse, but in those days it was the only way to fish the surf.

Then one day, when we were visiting Grampa at his huge house on Route 28, he showed us his newest fishing gear. Grampa always liked to have the newest technology (he owned the first car in Chatham). The pride and joy of Grampa's new fishing equipment was an almost straight bamboo pole with a strange-looking, cylindrical contraption strapped to its side.

The pole itself was a revolutionary leap ahead for surf fishers. With its length (about ten feet) and resilience, a much smaller lure could be sent out over the ocean, and sent out much further with far less effort. No longer would the heavy drail have to be whirled around over the head for the prodigious heave.

The second revolutionary breakthrough was the strange-looking cylinder on the side of the rod. Those first reels were called "knuckle dusters" with good reason. The handle spun backwards at great speed on the cast; knuckles and fingers would get a painful drubbing if you didn't pay strict attention. Those early reels didn't have any built-in drag, just a leather flap to press against the revolving line. The harder you pressed the more you slowed down the fish. But no longer did the line have to be arrayed so painstakingly on the beach.

And the line itself was different. This new material was linen, a strong, very thin line. This alone was a vast improvement on the old tarred cotton line. No longer did the fisherman's fingers have to get a coating of tar every time he went fishing.

It was all very primitive by today's standards, but it was a vast step forward from the old heaving and hauling—a step we all embraced with enthusiasm. More improvements came with time, but none have equaled that quantum leap from line arrayed on the beach to line wound on a reel.

In the late 1940s and early 1950s, when I was in my late teens and early twenties, we fished entirely from Monomoy's east-facing beaches. My generation first fished with the Calcutta or Tonkin cane poles that my grandfather had discovered. We wound on our own guides to take advantage of the irregularities in the bamboo poles. It was very much a do-it-yourself project, lining up the guides and affixing the reel in just the right location. But as technology permitted we succumbed to mass production and machine-made poles and switched over to the new, fiberglass poles. There was no question that the new fiberglass poles were better. They were straight where the cane poles were anything but. They were uniformly strong where the cane poles were not. The new poles were a step up, no question about it. They had plenty of whip, the snap that sends the lure rocketing out over the surfline.

With the old bamboo poles it was a minor art form to determine

78

which side of the pole was most advantageous to wind on the line guides. Each pole had a unique bend. The new fiberglass poles didn't have to be examined to determine which side would give the best cast. They were all perfectly straight. All they lacked was character. They were all the same. But they worked and worked well, although some of the early models were questionable.

Once, while demonstrating the virtues of a new fiberglass pole (I, too, like the newest things) to some friends who were still using cane poles, I flexed it to show off its superior resilience. As if to scorn my artful demonstration of the new technology, my pride and joy shattered in a dozen pieces. Maybe cane wasn't so bad after all. But bad or good, the cane poles did little but gather dust after the introduction of those new fiberglass rods.

Using the new poles we could make what we thought were some pretty lengthy casts. But these casts were prodigious only in our frame of reference. In the early 1950s on Monomoy's south end, we met some surf casters from Virginia who demonstrated true championship casting skill. These men had heard of Monomoy's fish-rich rips and came up to have a try at the fall run of brawny stripers. We thought we were hot stuff in the casting department, but their casts were home runs to our bunts.

After we enthused over the sheer beauty of their arching casts, they were nice enough to teach us their techniques. It was no surprise that, like any athletic endeavor, their skill was a combination of a lot of practice and careful attention to detail, particularly rewinding the line on those revolving spool reels. We had the practice part down pat; it was the exquisite care in the rewinding we needed to refine. Their techniques vastly improved our casts for the few years before spinning reels came into vogue. Once spinning reels became popular, the old revolving spool reels like my reliable Penn Squidder went the way of the cane poles — on the shelf. I still bring mine out now and then, give it a whirl or two to make sure it still works, marvel at the thumb-worn side where the chrome has been completely worn off by thousands of repetitions of use, then put it back lovingly in its box. This was no article of planned obsolescence. It always worked well and works well yet, fifty years after Ed Keene picked it up for me in some cut-rate store in Providence. That was a well spent $12.50.

Fishing always involved contests: who could get the most or the biggest; who could cast the furthest; whose car could go through the softest sand or go the fastest on the way to the "hot" spots. But while these were contests, they were unspoken, informal contests. We just watched the surf fisherman next to us and tried to outcast him. We didn't want to show off as much as we wanted to outcast whoever it was. We would see someone stuck in some sugar sand and then we would drive right through it without pause, and again, without mentioning it. Of course, sometimes in the doing we would get stuck right beside the original stickee and then the one-upmanship backfired mightily. Contests sure, but no one "let on." It was yesterday's way of being "cool."

Occasionally though, the contests would become more serious. There was a spell when some boat owners from over Harwich way made life a bit difficult for us. One summer it seemed that every evening schools of bluefish would gather just offshore and gradually work their way in to the beach where we could reach them with our casts from shore. Two or three of the boat people discovered the fish moving in on the beach and naturally decided they, too, would like to catch a few. And why not? But these floating fishermen had a "dog in the manger" type of personality. Rather than fish the ocean side of the schooled fish and letting us fish the inshore side of the same school, they drove the fish offshore out of our reach and reveled in our curses and raised fists. They knew we couldn't do anything about it. After a couple of evenings of this frustrating fishing, we came up with an anti-boat defense.

The next evening the same scenario presented itself—the bluefish gradually working in toward shore and those devilish Harwich boats coming in close to cut them off. There were three of us surf fishing that evening and this time we were ready for those Harwich Hairleggers. We waited until two of the boats were within range, replaced our lures with four-ounce pyramidal lead sinkers, and cast right at them. One boat was only about fifty feet away. Two of those lead weights hit the windshield and shattered it beyond redemption. The second boat escaped with dents in its woodwork and the occupants cowering below the gunnels. The tables were turned. Their boats were inboards; they couldn't come ashore. Curses and raised fists came from the other side with that encounter. Never again did those boats come between the fish and shore, at least while we were around.

Another year we had a similar situation facing us, that of catchable fish moving in close to the beach and some clown trying his best to drive them away. He was too far offshore for us to resort to a sinker stratagem. But, once in a while, circumstances occur that are aptly fitting. Again we were shaking our fists, yelling at this joker to fish the outside of the school, to let us have a crack at the fish, too. He just laughed—until his engine died. The schooling fish moved past the now quiet boat and moved right up to the beach, where we had a field day catching them and watching our tormentor with the engine hatch up, slowly drifting west into Nantucket Sound. The sun set, the fish kept biting, and the boat kept silent as it bobbed away toward Martha's Vineyard into the gathering gloom. It was a pretty sight.

Usually, the boat fisherman were gentlemen. They fished the outside of the schools; we fished the shore side, and we both prospered. It's human nature to exclaim over the misdeeds of others. For some strange reason we choose not to mention the vast majority of our encounters with our own kind that leave us feeling at the very least neutral and often leave us feeling all the better for the encounter. Why? If its human nature, perhaps we had better think about changing the facet of our behavior that accentuates the rare unpleasantness and concentrate instead on the plentiful contacts that produce the good feelings.

Just being on the island is usually enough to bring good feelings to the fore, and it was not at all unusual for this finger of sand to offer up a welcome surprise.

Monomoy's fringing, tide-lashed shoals make dramatic sights. The blue water and the white crashing surf are all overlain with the continuous thunderous roar of tumbling water. Seething, wave-tossed waters interposed with the undulating blue of the ocean beyond are an arresting sight no matter how often it is seen.

There is more to be gleaned from these waters than spectacular scenery, though. The big brawny bass and the lithe, fighting bluefish know to take advantage of these turbulent waters to feast on the baitfish struggling to maintain equilibrium. Fishermen, too, know to take advantage of these roiled waters for the big fish that are usually there.

Point Rip, Monomoy's south tip, is the epitome of tide-lashed shoals. This dramatic, wave-tossed, end of Monomoy is where Ed Keene and I, in the fall of 1949, discovered a type of fish we had never seen before. As we unlimbered our poles, we could see large, silvery fish slicing through the cresting waves, backlit against the setting sun. And not just one or two; there were numbers of whatever they were—something new to us. These fish were much too fast to be stripers, but we had no idea what they could be. They were also much easier to catch than bass, weighed about ten to fifteen pounds, and put up a terrific fight. They were a fledgling fisherman's fantasy, but what were these sleek, silvery fish with dramatic yellow eyes and rows of sharp, pointed teeth? It took a trip to the fish market for us to realize we had met the first bluefish to come back to these shores in many years. It was a fish we had heard about and had never seen. But not for want of trying.

The bluefish now come back earlier and earlier and are the backbone of a thriving charter fishery. Bluefish are a near perfect fish. They are fairly easy to catch, ferocious fighters, and are particularly tasty when broiled. Another gift of the ocean.

For us, our introduction to this oceanic gift was fishing perfection. It was a dramatic introduction to a dramatic fish.

A few years after that delightful discovery, when bluefish were regular fare at the Point, we decided the camp's larder could do with a fish or two. Fresh bluefish fillets broiled over open coals are the ocean's equivalent of filet mignon. We fired up the old car and headed for our usual fish pantry, Point Rip, stretching a mile or more towards Nantucket's Great Point, eleven miles away. This rip would usually produce fish (it still does) and if it didn't, it was always a spectacular spot (it still is).

Ed Keene was much more serious about life than I, but he was always a good companion and game for anything. We'd driven the bumpy outside (oceanside) ruts and the soft inside (through the dunes) road many times. On this trip we thought we would do a little cross-country exploration and make a new route to vary the experience somewhat. We would drive the blowouts.

What we called blowouts were the long, 400- or 500-yard depressions, located some twenty or thirty feet below the grassy dunes. These hollows were studded with fist-sized stones. The whistling winds of Monomoy kept vegetation from getting a foothold and also removed the lighter fine sand. What was left was a nearly flat, gravel-bottomed bowl.

As a footnote to this tale, I have since found out that these gravelly bottoms are an excellent place to look for Native American artifacts. Nature has rather obligingly and gently removed the extraneous sand, leaving the heavier objects arrayed as if on a table.

For us in those teenage years though, these flat-bottomed bowls were a fine place to exercise the normally slow-moving beach cars. Down in those stone-floored depressions we could reach the dizzying speeds of thirty or forty miles an hour. There were two heart-stopping spots. One was dropping into one of these chasms, the other when exiting the gulch. The car would be thrashing along in waist-high beach grass and all of a sudden, the earth would seemingly open up under us, the front end of the car would disappear, and we were headed straight down. We soon learned that the faster we approached the edge, the more precipitous the drop. This became a great way to initiate girls into the mysteries of the beach (and ourselves into the mysteries of the girls). When the car dropped off the edge it was usually accompanied by a scream of sheer terror as the female passenger, sure she was experiencing her last day on this earth, clutched the driver in a death grip. For awkward adolescents this became a quick and dramatic way to achieve closeness.

It didn't always work that way, though. One of my neophyte passengers apparently thought that jumping overboard was the lesser of the terrors (she didn't know I was harmless). Just as the roadster went over the edge, she leapt out, rolled thirty feet down the dune face, and came up sand-covered and angry. My ploy for getting next to this delightful girl failed miserably. Come to think of it, this method of impressing the girls never did work. All it did was impress us; the girls thought we were crazy.

What made the drop so sudden was the overhang. The beach grass roots formed a dense interwoven mat, and when the sand blew away under this tangled grass mat, the result was an overhanging shelf. When the front wheels of the car went across this shelf, it gave way. The drop was nearly vertical and instantaneous.

Dropping into one of these 30-to-40-foot deep depressions was simple. It was getting out that posed the bigger problem. The overhang that made the sudden descent so exciting was a major obstacle to the escape. Over time we became inured to the seeming hazards of the drop, but never did we become blase about the exiting.

As we sped across the bottom of one of these sand valleys, we gauged the slope and overhang of the proposed escape route. At full throttle, usually in second gear, we would ram the old car up that steep slope, through the least of the dreaded overhang, the car heading straight for the heavens, seemingly on the verge of going over backwards. Grass, roots, and barrels of flying sand would form a corona around the sky-ward-bound car. Then the hood would drop, the car would be back on level ground, ready for the next ordeal, and our heartbeat would return to its normal exhilarated pace.

Only a few cars could endure this abuse. I once tried using a 1938 Chevy in these blowouts. As the car bottomed out in the cup-shaped depression, both rear springs snapped and there she sat until we mounted a rescue mission a few weeks later.

Ford V-8s seemed to be the best. They could get up the speed necessary to fly up the exiting slope, push through the grassy roots, and still function. Their springs never broke. I'm sure the Ford company's engineers never envisioned their products in their second life regularly surviving such abuse, but I'm so glad they built in that extra measure of ruggedness. What fun they gave us.

But on this particular trip to the Point Rip, Ed and I decided to explore some new blowouts. An unexplored crater dead ahead had the usual precipitous drop and seemed particularly deep and long.

The trip along the base of the hole in second gear, throttle floored, made our ears ring and our hair fly. With the unmuffled car going flat out, we hit the least of the overhang with tremendous force, burst through in a flurry of sand and grass roots, and immediately found ourselves on just as steep a downslope covered with bayberry bushes.

What appeared to be two-to-three foot high plants were in reality ten- to fifteen-foot high mini-trees. The land really dropped away under these bushes. Only the tops were at a uniform level, pruned by the harsh, salt-laden winds of Monomoy. Unknowing, we crashed into the bayberries and were unwittingly hoisted on our own petard. The car easily crashed over the flanking bushes, but the momentum stopped when the bigger bushes, the ones that towered above us, lifted the driving wheels, all the wheels, off the ground.

Visibility was nonexistent; the vegetation was much higher than the car and we couldn't even open the doors. Those tree-sized, treelike trunks held them firmly shut. Suspended as she was, my poor old car was more like a tree house than a vehicle.

The fish would have to wait (the fishermen too). We had to come back to earth. In thinking about this adventure I'm sure we were as much surprised as imperiled. Neither of us, after a lifetime of fooling around on Monomoy's campus, had the slightest idea that bayberry bushes grew to such Olympian size.

After we got through laughing at our predicament, the first order of business was to extricate ourselves from our woodsy prison. There was only one way out and we took it; clad only in bathing suits, we crawled out the windows. Bayberries don't have thorns, but they do have short stiff branches that do a very good job of scraping off small bits of flesh from those who crawl, nearly naked, through them. The revenge of the bayberries?

It was a three-mile trek in soft beach sand back to the camp for axes, saws, and crowbars, then a return three-mile slog back to the car for the real work. Hacking a crude road out of the patch was no problem. The width of the brush-filled gully was only fifty feet or so. What turned out to be a major struggle was getting the car back down to the ground. We had to wiggle under the suspended car and cut out the stout, tree-like bushes that suspended it. This process brought back some vivid sandy/snowy memories from years before. Eventually, by dint of some fast slitherings and amid ominous creaking and cracking of breaking limbs, plus a few more scrapes and scratches, the old car noisily returned to its rightful place on this earth, with at least three of its wheels on the ground. A little back and forth, some more crunching and crackling, and we were out of the leafy impoundment and on the way to Point Rip.

Only the fact that we had started out to go fishing carried us to the Rip. There were many sore spots on our bodies, and we had walked six hot miles in soft beach sand. Our "fishing" that day mostly consisted of sitting against the old car, watching the surf, and letting the warm summer sun have its healing way with our scratched, scraped, bruised, and tired bodies.

I recently walked the same dune edge where Ed and I had parted the bushes and gotten our comeuppance. Now, fifty years later, our cuts and scratches have long since healed, the black-and-blue spots have long since disappeared. However, the slot we made in that bayberry forest is still plainly visible. The dune top is still there. Point Rip still seethes in the distance, and the fish are still waiting to be caught. On today's walks along that same dune face, just a glimpse of that swath mowed in the bayberry bushes brings back in full the rich flavor of our day in Monomoy's only version of a forest.

Bayberry bushes aren't the only hazard on the beach. Monomoy is a place where mosquitoes have honed the duties of survival to a fine art. While their hordes don't darken the skies, they dim the brightness of a summer day considerably. My uncle and I were at the very southern tip of Monomoy, fishing the always wild waters of Point Rip. The bluefish were there in numbers. We both hooked up on our first cast and were looking forward to some exciting action.

So apparently were Monomoy's mosquitoes. They saw us as a meal of ample proportions and we were amply displayed—the only red blood for miles around. They made the most of it. The gentle northeast wind pushed the buzzing swarms of those bloodsucking insects down on us as bees go to nectar. No, more like iron filings to a magnet. For the first and only time in my life, we cut off hooked fish and ran for the car to escape.

Well, sort of an escape. On the ten-mile drive off the beach, the exhaust pipe fell off the beach buggy in one of the few grassy sections of beach and set the tinder-dry grass on fire. This occurred just north of one of the camps. We couldn't let it burn itself out; it would very likely consume the camp. So we stopped. It was a very hot day and my uncle already had welts from a particularly bad case of the hives, and major itches from the mosquito's bites—exacerbating the disappointment of having to leave the Rip full of fish. To add to his very real discomfort, the sweat trickling over the itches and the hives made the poor man nearly berserk. The fire was eventually put out, but during our efforts I noticed that the air around my uncle's head was a shade bluer than any-where else on the island. I noticed, too, that he didn't ask to be taken down to Monomoy for a fishing trip for a good long time afterward.

We did a lot of surf casting along that magnificent stretch of beach, and with the arrival of the fighting bluefish, we also did a lot of fish catching. There is something soul satisfying about standing on a lonely wave-lapped beach on the edge of the continent with a fishpole in hand. I now sense that standing on the shore with a fish pole in hand was more an excuse to admire the ocean's many moods than an attempt to stock the larder. As I mentioned earlier, it was probably my Yankee heritage that wouldn't let me just enjoy the sensations that ocean gazing brings; somehow I had to be productive too. Or at least make the pretense of being productive—productive pretense.

Ed and Westy Keene, two brothers who bracketed me in age, were good friends. Ed usually caught more fish than I. He stuck to it. Ed also had luck riding on his shoulder, fisherman's luck. Fisherman's luck is a little-understood phenomenon but it exists—any fisherman will attest to that. People afflicted with this condition always bring home more fish than their unafflicted brethren. For the vast majority of us not so blessed, it is often a frustrating situation. On one trip down by the Stonehorse Lightship, Ed and I spotted a batch of terns in frenzied pur-suit of surfacing bait, a good sign of larger fish below. We hopped out of the old car, grabbed our poles, and headed for the low surf. I made a beautiful arching cast right over the school of bait. Ed's cast started in a similar fashion, arching out over the ocean; then zap, the dreaded back-lash, and his lure snapped back to bullet into the surf, right at his feet. We went off the beach that day with one fish, a nice, fat thirty-three-pounder; Ed caught it on that backlashed cast. Fisherman's luck is hard to beat.

***

Cape Cod's east flank presents a fifty-mile shelving beach to the ocean. Occasionally something other than sand decorates this clean, outer coast. Once in awhile dead whales are soggily deposited on our catch-all shores.

This random stranding of whale carcasses once provided opportunity for a beleaguered fishing crew on Monomoy.

In the late 1940s, two small groups of men from off-Cape had an intense but not very serious rivalry. The contest concerned fish, specifically striped bass. Whichever crew tallied the most fish at year's end had to host a dinner for the other. The good doctor's crew, through luck, perseverance, and perhaps a little better knowledge of the vagaries of the tide rips, somehow managed to come home with a few more fish than their friends. They were the clear leaders in the piscatorial competition.

September is one of the best months to fish the Rip. The big bass are furiously feeding, stocking up for the long migration south. Both groups of the friendly fishermen knew this (any Cape Cod fisherman knows this), so they usually arranged to take their vacations at their camps close by the obliging Point Rip during this fish friendly month.

The doctor's group woke in the predawn darkness to make their usual foray to the Rip half a mile distant. When they pushed against the camp's only door, it wouldn't open. It acted as though something was holding it shut. Something was.

During the night, while they slept, some of the crew from the other camp had come across a dead male sperm whale washed up on the outer beach. Thinking to slow down their friends' lead in the competition, they had removed that part of the whale which unmistakably proclaims male (a part some six feet long). They then screwed (so as not to waken the sleepers) this rawhide-like strip of flesh across the door of the doctor's camp.

* * *

Live whales are fairly common around the Cape in the warmer months and always delight us with their proximity. They surge north by the Cape in April, and a careful observer in November might see the telltale spouts misting the ocean as the great beasts head south. On the rare occasions when these animals deign to move in along the beaches; the sight is at once awe inspiring and at the same time, humbling.

While driving to the camp on an Easter weekend, we were treated to a once-in-a-lifetime sight. Perhaps once in many lifetimes. As we pulled out on the open beach, a large black object lazily appeared out of the water about 200 yards offshore—too close for a submarine, too small for a boat. Whatever it was slowly disappeared. For a few seconds it was as though fantasy had replaced reality. The next act quickly dispelled such thoughts. Rising slowly, majestically out of the ocean came the unmistakable tail of Poseidon's finest—a whale, a stone's throw from the beach. I'd never seen a whale so close to the shore. This creature was at least fifty feet long; its length equalled the height of a five-story building. The feeling of humility brought on by the close observation of this gentle leviathan was soon eclipsed by the reason for this rare shoreside appearance. Here were two whales. It was spring, and courtship was on their minds. Languid motions, slow surface rolls, fins, tails, great surges of water—it was a titanic and lazily insistent courtship. The two great beasts were engaged in the most elemental ritual to the slow beat of nature's tympanic symphony.

Their explosive exhalations had a hollow echoing sound, a resonant whoosh one could imagine coming down a long corridor from a far distant time. They were sighs of celebration, of life—sighs for new life for these scarce survivors.

It seemed entirely appropriate that these great animals on the razor's edge of extinction should be initiating life on a day when the Christian world celebrated the rising of Christ.

If all proceeded as nature intended, a baby right whale would enter the world in about twelve months. Perhaps what we witnessed will be repeated enough times so that future generations won't have to exclaim over the rare sightings of these endangered giants. Rather, the sightings will become commonplace—noteworthy only because nature's handiwork is so magnificently displayed.

A Most Joyous Henhouse

Monomoy, like the mainland, has seasons, but on the island, seasons are accentuated. Winter beach memories centered around our snug little camp. It was an eight- by twelve-foot building I was given the use of for many years. A little building that started its life as my grandparents' hen house in South Chatham, then was flaked (taken apart in sections) and moved to Monomoy. This building in its Monomoy years heard more laughter and saw more pure pleasure than most buildings ever see. It was a most joyful henhouse.

Out on that bleak, windswept beach, the camp was a particularly cozy oasis of heat and life. What made the camp a pleasure to be in was a cast-iron range, a Glenwood. This was a magnificent piece of a stove maker's art. Glenwoods were built right here in Massachusetts and they were built to last.

Ours had trained me well in the feeding of its prodigious appetite. The first order of business in rousing the cold cast iron was to stuff the firebox with paper and kindling, flip the kindle/bake lever to kindle, throw in a match, and wait for the cast iron to warm up. There would be pings and pops, the crackle of burning wood, and the occasional loud crack of expanding metal—stove waking-up noises. Peeking out from the heat- warped lids, winking furiously, would be the orange eye of that friendly fire coming to life. After a period of time, and only experience would tell you when, the lever was shifted to bake. If you misjudged the timing, the stove quickly told you so in no uncertain terms. Smoke gushed from every crack and crevice, a sure sign you had switched to bake when "Big Black" was still in the kindle frame of mind. If you tried to hurry the process, it was no contest. The hulking Glenwood won every time.

On the other hand, if you judged the timing correctly, the stove would settle down to do its job. There would be a cheerful little chorus of stove noises as it heated the camp, the occupants, and the food in its care.

A marvelous invention, that Glenwood range. You never felt alone at the camp. The old stove was good company, with its winking eye, its exuberant noises, and its smoke-threatening ways.

Memories of the camp in winter are etched deeply in my mind, particularly winter meals. All kinds of meals from the island's many food sources come to mind. One of the best I've ever experienced is an oyster stew at camp. The day's foraging would begin at the Hospital (a small tidal pond at Inward Point) at low tide, with hip boots and quahog rake. The goal was to gather enough oysters, eight or ten per person, for a stew. That done, we would repair to the camp a half mile distant and coax the old Glenwood to life.

As the small building warmed, the windows would bead with condensation. The furniture would slowly trade its accumulated cold for the more tolerable heat of the stove.

Over by the sink, the day's catch would be opened; hopefully the temptation to slurp a few of those delicious oysters would be resisted by the opener. Should the temptation not be resisted, a few threatening growls and dire threats would be heard from the waiting hungry.

When the fire was going well and the camp was well along on the path to warmth, it was time to put together the scant ingredients for the stew. Generally, this didn't take much time, but the whole project would have taken the better part of the day, a delightful part of the day. The light cream was heated in a double boiler arrangement until it was good and hot. Then the oysters and some of their liquor were added. When the oyster's edges had curled in their warm salty bath, it was about time to belly up to the table.

The heavy, crazed milkstone bowls with the steaming white stew, the swirls of melted, yellow butter, an occasional white oyster breaking the surface, and over all a sprinkling of red paprika was an ocean-inspired palette of glorious design. Bathe it all in the soft yellow light of the kerosene lanterns, add the shriek and moan of the cold north wind whistling around the camp's corners, and you have a sensory-fulfilling memory of the best.

And by now, the camp would be good and warm, warm enough to make tall candles sag and tall men wilt—just about right for those that had been wading around scratching up the oysters out there in the frigid moaning wind. They probably still had a heat deficit.

Those bowls of stew would satisfy any appetite and set a high mark for seafood excellence. They also set the stage for somnolence for the eaters. When the meal was about over the contemplation began; the memory of that cold, biting wind was fading fast. Maybe it wasn't all that bad getting those oysters after all. It had taken awhile to fire up the old stove and get the camp warmed, but what really mattered was the taste of those oysters, the warmth of the camp, and the pleasure of sharing the best with friends. The essence of the trip was well worth the experience of the harvest. As always.

The memories of my Monomoy experiences were usually imbued with a luster that mainland experiences rarely attain. Perhaps it's because they happened a long time ago. Perhaps it's the mind's ability to patina yesterday's experiences with an extra soft glow. Whatever the reason, the luster remains and the glow seems brighter with time.

Nature's crop—the oysters, clams, and other shellfish—were just part of Monomoy's offerings. The beach, with some help from man, produced many of the props for our numerous schemes. We were into recycling long before recycling became a popular thing. We called it scrounging and practiced it continually, perfecting the art. Scrounging is apparently a lifetime addiction, maybe an affliction. All of my three sons are so afflicted.

During the early desperate years of the Second World War, Monomoy Island itself was called on to contribute to our country's gigantic, burgeoning war effort. The midsection of the island, just south of Inward Point was designated a bombing and strafing target. An enormous shallow wood and sand pyramid was built and painted white, and oiled roads were laid in the form of concentric rings—from the air, a gigantic bull's-eye for fledgling bombers. Eventually, three sets of paired railroad rails with hooks welded on them sprouted on the beach. We couldn't imagine what they might be until we heard the staccato blasts of aerial machine gun fire and later saw the dimples in the upright rails. The rails were supports for strafing targets which were hung on the hooks by the Coast Guardsmen. The global war was inching closer and closer to our souls.

Then, strangest of all, a giant tin can lying on its side appeared on the beach. It was about ten feet long and about eight feet in diameter, open at both ends and made of half-inch sheet steel. It looked like a small steel cave. And that's what it proved to be.

This latest, and by far the strangest, addition to the array of targets, came at a time when our troops in Europe were trying to dislodge the enemy from caves by a newly established aerial technique called skip bombing, a way to deliver bombs horizontally.

This big can was a cave-sized target for the flyers to hone their skip bombing skills. I hadn't thought about it till now, but while the idea was workable in conception, it must have been all but invisible from the bomber's vantage, end on. I wonder if any bombs ever zipped through.

This rusting cylinder sat on the beach for two or three years after the war. Then one of us had a wonderful inspiration that, as the camp need-ed a new outhouse, perhaps this fake cave could be utilized. It certainly wasn't doing any good where it was. We would bring the thing to the camp, stand it on end on a dune top, put a cover over it, and build the outhouse on the cover. We would have a fantastic lookout tower and the greatest facility on the beach, all in one fell swoop. Once the can was in place we would paint the thing to resemble a Campbell soup can. We were going to be Pop artists long before Pop artistry became popular. To our eyes, in our minds, at that time, this would be a stellar addition to this otherwise pristine beach. The possibility that it would be an eyesore never occurred to us.

It would be practical, too, and Cape Codders tend to be practical with a capital "P". The capacity would be infinite, the view stupen-dous—a room with a view and then some. We might even have to charge admission. It would be a throne worthy of a king and we, mere mortals, would be using it. Our eyes would be taking in the softly curv-ing, sweeping dune lines, the snow-white sands, the gentle green grass-es, and the dark blueberry bushes of Wildcat Swamp replete with the scolding, red-winged blackbird. And over across the swamp would be the surf-fringed Atlantic stretching to the horizon. Majesty is where you find it.

Another one of our schemes involved raising the stern half of the Pendleton.

In February, 1952, a northeaster of magnificent proportions swept in and snapped two 10,000-ton tankers in half. The stern half of one, the Pendelton, lay grounded a half mile or so offshore of the island, taunting us with its proximity. Inflated rumors of its value swirled around town for years, like Chatham fog. We kids, like everyone else, came up with all manner of schemes to salvage the hulk. Jim Eldredge, a close friend and fellow disciple of Monomoy, who was probably a relation but a very distant one, since he was an "e" Eldridge, had the most original idea for floating the Pendleton—load her up with an infusion of ping pong balls. Fortunately, none of us knew a ping pong ball manufacturer nor could we afford ten million ping pong balls. Not only would that idea have worked, but we could have sold the ping pong balls that did the lifting, as souvenirs. That particular plan remained on the shelf. Alas.

The scheme to salvage the huge tin can though, stayed on the front burner. It was a beautiful summer day when we put our planning into action. A perfect day for just such a project.

Six of us gathered at the site for the big move, a crowd by Monomoy standards. The sight that greeted us was somewhat more daunting than we had remembered. This cylinder had been sitting in place for eight to ten years, and that place was a marshy swamp. It had settled in nicely, in about a foot of water and mud. All the surfaces inside and out were resplendent with a thick, scaly crust of rust, not at all surprising in Monomoy's salt-laden air. What we hadn't thought about, hadn't really seen till now, were the multitudes of holes—bullet holes. Apparently, the aerial gunners got bored shooting at their regular gunnery targets and decided to riddle the big drum. This added a substantial hazard to the moving operation. Inside and out, this huge cylinder resembled nothing so much as a giant cheese grater. Where the bullets went in there was a nicely dimpled hole, but where they came through, splayed, jagged shards of steel waited to take a bite out of the unwary. No matter. It wouldn't affect our use of the thing; indeed, the perforations would add some much-needed ventilation. We would just have to be more careful in the moving.

We (all six of us) got in the steel tunnel and like gerbils on the exercise wheel, ran up the sides a time or two. It gave enough to let us know it was moveable, that maybe our idea would work and we could move it out of that swamp.

Rust is annoying. It stains your hands, it dulls your saw blades, and down your neck, it itches. None of us had ever been in a rust rain before, but when that rust-crusted object started to stir, we all instantly became covered and caked with rust. We became rust dust inhalers of the first magnitude. What a mess. It took a fair bit of cajoling and many bribes on my part to entice the crew back inside the shedding drum. Once again, like gerbils, we took our places in the rusty cylinder and started the rocking action. The rust rain continued unabated as we worked the drum back and forth in its longtime bed, each effort bringing it fractionally closer to freedom.

After one final prodigious effort, a fresh shower of rust, and some sucking noises, the drum started to roll. With the first half-revolution the rust rain was as nothing compared to the six inches of mud, rotted leaves, and dead vegetation that had slowly rotated with the drum until it was directly overhead. Gravity triumphed and down it came, the six- or eight-year accumulation of the black watery muck right on our heads. We were a sorry-looking sight as we emerged from the big can, our bodies stained red from the rust with a nice thick coating of black mud dripping from every part of our anatomy. There was no audience save ourselves, no call for an encore.

But the messy work was done and at this point we couldn't get any dirtier. It was just a matter of getting the old beach car behind the thing to push it back to the camp three miles away. Now that it was out of its long time bed it moved very easily. We backed the car up to the cylinder and tried an experimental push or two. It moved to the accompaniment of loud grindings and metallic screeches, as the rusty sides of the revolving drum with the bullet hole protrusions scraped and gouged the bumper and trunk of the car. The driver couldn't see where to go. Through the rear window there was a revolving wall of rust, and we were going backwards. But it was the only way we could move the thing. If we had tried to push the darned thing, those splayed fingers of bullet-punctured steel would have torn the radiator to shreds in an instant. Two of us flanked the car by about twenty-five feet off each side and directed the driver around the biggest obstacles. It worked pretty well once we got the hang of how to turn the thing.

If the push was on the middle of the drum it went fairly straight, a push on either end and the drum pivoted. And all of this motion was accompanied by the most awful cacophony of revolving dry metal scraping on stationary dry metal. It seemed as if the drum was rejoicing in its motion. Inside the car though, it was as if 10,000 banshees had been let loose with the sole object of deafening us with their demonic wails.

We were slowly getting closer to our goal, the high dune by the camp. The last obstacle was the marsh flanking the Romp Hole Creek (how was that creek named?), a place the scratched and scraped car couldn't go. By now the crew was quite exhilarated with the whole adventure. It looked like the end was near. We performed our treadmill act once again to effortlessly cruise across the marsh, but we were stopped at the creek. Its five-foot width defeated all our efforts. We just didn't have the weight to roll the drum out of this final hole, and we couldn't get the car close enough to use its power.

We just sat and looked at it for some time; it was so close to our goal. After all that effort, we were stopped. It was discouraging. I think at that point we were all beginning to realize the enormity of the project we had undertaken, and at least some of us (me) felt relieved that the object of our efforts was immovable. It got us off the hook. It also rid some dune top of a future eyesore. All we had done was move the thing from one marsh to another, but we did have a singular adventure to talk about. We were discolored by rust dust to the point of anonymity, but the cave had been moved a couple of miles when the scoffers didn't think we could budge it an inch.

But the camp still needed an outhouse. Our dander was up. We were in an outhouse collecting mode. Somebody remembered seeing an outhouse on its side over in back of the abandoned Middle Station. If we couldn't move the target maybe we could scale down and salvage this newest offering. Sure enough, the hollow in the dune housed a tidy little one-holer that time had sterilized. It was, as advertised, abandoned and rather forlornly lying on its side, resting, as if it were just waiting to be put back in service. This moving job was, comparatively, a piece of cake. We hooked the roof of the little building over that badly scraped rear bumper, put all the crew in the back of the car to give the tires plenty of purchase, and dragged it back to the camp to another hollow on the very edge of Wildcat Swamp, where it sat for the rest of its days. We found an ancient telephone at the dump, the kind with a fixed mouthpiece mounted on a boxlike contraption and a hand cranked bell. We mounted this inside as a receptacle for the paper and scrounged an old sign for a telephone booth, which we tacked up on the outside. Ever after, when the need arose, it was, "I have to make a call."

Droll humor, Monomoy style.

Monomoy attracted characters much as a magnet attracts iron filings. Our camp's occasional neighbor, an elderly woman named Daisy, came down for a part of each summer. And as long as her camp was extant she continued to spend part of each summer out on the island. A tough lady, she lived to 104 and by all accounts chopped her own kindling for nearly all of that time. She seemed to stay pretty much to herself, but as we discovered, such was not always the case. One very still night there came a soft knock at the door. In the quiet of the summer's evening this was most unusual. There were obviously no cars around; we hadn't heard a sound. Did Monomoy ghosts knock? It turned out to be our neighbor. Apparently she had been using our facility for some time, but only in the dark of night. We hadn't been aware. She wanted to know if she could use the facility and also, could she borrow some paper for same. We told her to borrow the outhouse anytime she felt the desire (an apparently unnecessary instruction) but she could have the paper.

On another occasion she came over to "borry" (her word) our ladder. She had some shingles that needed replacing. She was going to do the repair job herself because she didn't want her fifteen-year-old grandson climbing around on the roof of the place. He might hurt himself. She was in her mid-eighties at the time. Daisy was into self-reliance long before it was an "in thing."

I have never thought of Cape Codders as trendsetters but in retrospect I can see that with our recycling, with our do-it-ourselves projects, our attempts at Pop Art and Daisy's spirit of independence, we were blazing a trail for the rest of the nation. The nation didn't know it, we didn't know it, but there we were, out in the forefront, just waiting for the nation to catch up. Ah, the majesty of it all.

Cape Cod's characters were thick on the ground in the postwar years and had been for all of my life. Places like Monomoy not only attracted characters it nurtured them. Sad to say, they seem to be disappearing. It's a shame—these characters defined the parameters of our society. Our zeal toward the homogeneous is bearing bland fruit.

Part III
A Monomoy Finale

The Cape Codder Newspaper

As surely as the glaciers once came, people, too, came to the Cape in increasing numbers.

The increasing popularity and growth of our peninsula was evident on the pages of *The Cape Codder* newspaper. The Cape's sleepy ways were fast disappearing, though some evidence of those more casual times showed through, as this February 1, 1951, article reported:

> When Brewster folk talk about turtles and the old time art of turtling, the story is still told of the late Harry McAnistan who used to go turtling and keep them in his cellar until such time as he could ship them to the city market.
>
> One day the electric meter man came to read the meter which was situated in the cellar of the McAnistan home. Little did the man realize what he was walking into when he entered the cellar which at the time harbored fifty or more of the ill tempered snapping turtles. The meter man did not realize his predicament until he found himself virtually surrounded by the vicious snappers, but his fast legwork delivered him safely from the trap. Thereafter the meter man shunned the McAnistan cellar as he would a lion's den.

The article continued to report on the very few men still living who could find winter-bedded turtles. It is an article that illustrates the affinity the old-timers had for the natural world. The rhythms and nuances of nature were in no way lost on their generation. I don't hunger for the "good old days," but sometimes I would like to have a peek into the everyday life of three or four generations ago, to experience how they coped, how they did that which now seems impossible, like turtling. How did those people first discover how to find a turtle embedded in the cold winter mud? And what did they do with the creature once they had it in hand, so to speak? How hungry did they have to get before a snapping turtle looked like food?

In this same time period, the purveyors of skunk oil still had a market. An article attesting to its almost miraculous healing power was front page news. It cured a little girl's croup, and another sufferer, this time with a severe case of hoarseness, was able to speak without effort after one application. An old-timer with crippling rheumatism was able to lay away one of his two canes. Taken internally or externally it was purported to be the greatest cure for winter lameness extant.

Evidence of the increasing traffic on the Cape's roads was affecting even skunk oil production. A trapper, eighty-five-year-old John Silver of Yarmouthport, proclaimed," There ain't as many skunks as there used to be. The automobiles are killing them all off."

"Square rigger life was tough," read a March 3, 1949 headline. An old-timer who lived alone in West Chatham had spent some of his life on the last of the square riggers. He went to sea at age thirteen, a not uncommon thing in those days, and finally gave up on the life of an offshore sailor to become a local fisherman. He said there was "too darn much discipline and the food was none to good on those square riggers." He also clearly remembered the daily stagecoach that passed his house every day.

In a May 25, 1950 story, Edward L. Clark, former captain of the old Monomoy Point Life Saving Station, told about his years at that lonely spot. He proclaims that time in his life as the happiest time he ever spent in the service (Monomoy seems to work its magic on every generation). He told of the wrecks and of the travails during the rescues. He recalled the many shanties around the Powder Hole and how a school was established because so many fishermen brought their families to this little harbor at sea.

But not all the men on the sea in harm's way were fortunate enough to be rescued. Here is the January 2, 1950 story of two Chatham fishermen who were lost while bringing in their fish catches, destined mostly for the New York market.

They came in the entrance of Chatham harbor in one of those familiar Chatham fogs. The harbor entrance is wide enough. The channel is the hazard, it isn't dredged enough. The two Chatham fishermen hit the bar, their boat capsized and they were lost. Elroy M. Larkin was 54. Archer E Nickerson was 45. Archie was the father of five children. Roy leaves three children.

One of Roy's three children was a classmate of mine in high school. . . Over the years, two of my twenty-three classmates were called out of the classroom to learn the terrible news, the loss of their fathers to that gray, cold ocean.

Another headline (July 3, 1952) tied the old ways to the new: "First Message Since Nazis Came, Rides French Cable to Orleans." The transatlantic cable was back in operation for what was to be a fairly short time. War-stimulated technology was moving information sharing ahead in prodigious leaps. This nineteenth-century cable was soon to be abandoned, but ocean-spanning cables still snake across the wide Atlantic.

The outside world was intruding more and more into our Cape Cod lives. Halfway around the world they held a little war dubbed a police action and our boys (myself included) were being called to serve. Nearly every issue of the paper had pieces about the Cape's young men reporting for service or coming back from that cold, bleak land.

But this police action in which 59,000 of our country's young people met an untimely death was just a blip on the horizon of the Cape's development.

Shorefront land was becoming valuable. A piece in the paper marveled at how, just a short while before, beach property was so valueless that owners neglected to record their deeds. Times were changing. The woodlands, once the only land with any value, were now far less desirable than the formerly disdained beach front. The shore front land was started on an upward escalation that still, fifty years later, shows no sign of abating. Will Rogers' old adage, "They ain't making any more land," is very much in force on Cape Cod today. There are more and more of us with more and more money and less and less land to go around.

Each town on the Cape was (and still is) wrestling with serious conservation issues. The jury was out on how the Cape towns would fare in protecting that which made them desirable.

One Outer Cape town was having nothing to do with looking ahead. An article chronicling the delightful contrariness, individualism, and crankiness of some Cape Codders all came to the fore in the 1949 town meeting in Wellfleet. Half the town's 800 registered voters showed up. They deemed no fireworks for that year, and with what could be construed as a head in the sand inclination, voted down town planning. Wellfleet chose not to see the rampant overdevelopment that was ravaging the Upper Cape.

By September of that year an ad appeared that spoke directly to the changing mores of our nation's peoples. This full-page ad proclaimed in bold black letters: "ONLY YOU CAN PRESERVE YOUR TRAINS." It was the beginning of the end of an era of the inexpensive transportation that had served the Cape so well. The very ruralness of the Cape doomed the trains. It was all well and good to get here by rail, relaxing as well, but when you arrived on Cape, then what? Public transportation was somewhere well in the future—people needed a car when they arrived. Fewer and fewer people bothered with the train.

In 1949, the Cape was fortunate to have the services of a farsighted State Senator, Edward Stone. In October of that year, *The Cape Codder* reported his proposal to establish a two-year community college on Cape Cod. This was just the kind of thinking the Cape needed if it was to offer more than just a tourist economy. Fortunately for the Cape, we usually find some farsighted people to help work out that which is best in the long run, and largely, they have prevailed.

Two articles in the early 1950's surprised me with their worldly scope and underlying aroma of fear. One detailed the Communist Party line on Cape Cod. I hadn't realized that our little bit of heaven was under siege by Communists. Apparently the threat was real enough to provoke a lengthy article in the paper. The other article was even more revealing about the fears and apprehensions of that time. Titled, "Survival Under Atomic Attack," it reported on how to best survive a nuclear attack. I don't remember any such fears being expressed by those I knew, but the editor of the paper saw fit to give this instruction full page coverage.

On a more optimistic note, in the 1950's the increasingly numérous and sophisticated visitors to the Cape were treated to Broadway musicals with the opening of the Music Circus (now the Melody Tent), located in the west end of Hyannis. If ever one wanted proof that a seismic change was sweeping the Cape this was it. In those early times musicals were the order of the day. What a fortunate thing for us that these tented productions came to the Cape. We very provincial kids were now able to see the live shows we had been reading about. For me at least, this was a wonderful "open sesame" into a world I had only heard of. I don't think I missed a single show those first few years. Kiss Me Kate, Oklahoma, Guys and Dolls—they were all grist for my mill. Memories of those colorful musicals still bring a smile.

On February 8, 1951, *The Cape Codder* proclaimed, "Bird Slaughter On Cape Beaches." This was an annual occurrence: dead and dying birds washing up on the east-facing Cape Cod beaches. All during the war years we assumed the crude oil came from torpedoed ships off our coast and probably some of it did. But after the war the pathetic dead and dying birds kept coming up on our beaches. We later learned that tankers would flush their bilges off the coast and the oil slicks would move onshore on the easterlies and ensnare the birds that were only looking for a little calm water. I remember it as a hideous and common sight. I also wondered how many of these birds there must have been to take those tremendous losses year after year.

'No Problem'

Ispent every spare moment and all my spare cash on the upkeep of my first beloved old island, flivver. This car, purchased for $20 at a local junkyard, was a Model A—a perfect car for the beach, and a perfect car for neophytes to learn about car fixing. This most basic of cars had very few things that could go wrong. Things that occasionally did go awry often could be fixed on the spot. It was a most forgiving car, and at that stage in my vehicular education it needed to be.

In my single-minded passion for the joys of Monomoy, I once invited my bosses to take a car trip down the island. I was the low man on the totem pole, the "gofer" kid for the tedious work that didn't need much skill.

The Galvin brothers were two recent arrivals on the Cape. Like many others, they moved here for the building opportunities that opened up after World War ll. They were my employers for a summer or two during my high school years, good-humored men who taught a neophyte something about the building trade.

One of the cottages we put together had a fine view across Nantucket Sound to the shining sands of Monomoy Island. Across the five-mile stretch of dark blue waters, the gleaming white sands of that fingerlike island gleamed as always, like a beckoning beacon.

The call of those white sands was all but irresistible, and I kept talking up the wonders of the island until my bosses finally succumbed to my urgings and agreed we could take a summer afternoon off at pay. Their only condition was that we be back by five, our normal quitting time. I assured them that would be "no problem"; the trip I had planned would easily get us back by five. Right at lunchtime we set off for what I thought was their enlightenment, and what they probably thought was a way to shut me up.

Plans are so simple to make at age sixteen. It's only the results of these makeshift plans that bring on the complications and the education.

None of my three bosses were outdoor types. Their first query was, "Will we need shoes?"

I assured them that they wouldn't need shoes, that I never wore shoes on the beach. They were only going to be in the rowboat or the car. They wouldn't be doing any walking. Just leave the shoes behind.

We rowed across the cut-through by Horne's Cottages to the waiting, trusty Model A. Right away an omen (which in my excitement I ignored) presented itself. Someone had "borrowed" a vital part of my carburetor. Luckily, there was another similar car in the small grouping of beach cars. It took but a moment for me to "reborrow" this same vital part and re-attach it to my car (this was a common practice). We were ready.

All four cylinders roared to life, and my passengers' education on the wonders of Monomoy was about to begin. The thought that my educa-tion was also about to be revised never occurred to me. As we chugged up Coast Guard hill, I extolled on the magnificent views of the mighty Atlantic spreading to the horizon, the island stretching off to our right and barely visible in the distance, the abandoned lighthouse down near our furthest goal. I also noticed that the car seemed to be working much harder than it ever had. I had never carried this much weight in the car.

Cooling systems are designed to keep the engine cool, and in nor-mal use on hard-surfaced roads this is usually no problem. But by the time these worn-out cars arrived on the island, the cooling systems were clogged with the sediment of long use. Certainly they were not working at anywhere near their normal efficiency. Also, these cars had been fitted with much fatter tires than the designer had ever intended. This, cou-pled with the soft sands of the beach, meant these cars always labored. The harder they worked the hotter they ran. We countered this failing by carrying jugs of water to placate the steaming iron of the overworked engine. It was a simple solution—water was free and plentiful.

The trip down the beach, directly into the summer's southwesterlies, into the cooling and prevailing wind was rarely a problem. Trips off the beach, with the wind, were another story.

The old cars usually went about the same speed and the same direction as the gentle breezes. That meant there was no cooling air wafting through the radiator. A trip off the beach meant two or three stops to assuage the overheated engine. We became quite expert at turning the cars into the wind and emptying gallon jugs of water into steaming, erupting cauldrons.

As we progressed down the beach, my employers seemed to appreciate the beauty of this pristine bit of beach heaven. They succumbed to the vistas of snow-white sands sandwiched between the deep blue of the ocean, and the sweeping, rich green, grass-covered dunes, the whole scene capped with the light blue sky decorated with fluffy white cumulus clouds. These men had come from off Cape somewhere; such expanses of beach without a soul in sight were something they had never seen. They were probably feeling a little like kids playing hooky. None of their families knew they were out on that deserted beach. As we were to get back by quitting time they hadn't bothered to tell their wives about this expedition.

I pulled out on the outside beach and talked up Chatham Bars, plainly visible on our left. I told of the fearsome, turbulent waters where so many sailing vessels had come to grief. A little farther down the beach was Schooner Bar, a line of white water pointing to the northeast. I told them the bar was a great place for stripers. A mile or so south of Schooner Bar was the southern end of Chatham Bars, another place bass and bass fishermen seemed to congregate. It was the last bar of consequence until Point Rip at the end of the beach. I was talking up the beach and its manifold treasures and pleasures at a great rate and having a good time doing it. I really enjoyed showing off Monomoy (and still do). They, too, seemed to be enjoying the outing, so different from their normal, daily routine.

What I wasn't talking up was the fact that on this trip into the wind, the old car was overheating, something that had never happened before. We were all having a good time and there were plenty of water stops along the way. Portents are ignored by sixteen-year-olds. They don't exist until they hit hard.

My crew enthused about the magnificent high dunes near the end of the island, the inspirational free-form panorama of white sand and green grasses. From the top of one of these soaring dunes looking south we could just make out Nantucket peeking over the edge of the ocean, and to the north we could see the mainland of Cape Cod from Chatham to Hyannis.

From the visual landmarks we could even make out the area where we should have been working. This was all good stuff for my crew. They had never seen the Cape from across the water. They were puzzling out where their homes were in relation to the white church steeple that so clearly marks Harwichport. Cape Cod's cloud-raking steeples are exclamation marks of some note and easily identify our towns.

By now, the wind had ever so gently swung into the east and we were seeing the last of any long distance views. Like a veil of spider webs across the sunlit sky, some of that Chatham fog came silently off the always cold Atlantic, slid across the warm beach, and enveloped us. Monomoy had, as if shyly, displayed all we were to see. It was time to go.

We refilled all the water jugs in the abandoned Coast Guard Station cistern and headed for home, ten miles away. Monomoy had worked its usual magic.

The fog that afternoon was as thick as any I'd ever experienced. The windshield instantly beaded with moisture, but this was no real problem. There was only one inside road off the beach and we were on it. The boat was only ten miles away, straight up the ruts. It was four o'clock. We had to be back around five, "no problem."

Water was a problem though. The scant southeast wind meant no wind was wafting through the radiator. The cooling-off periods were coming at much shorter intervals, and it soon became obvious that we didn't have enough fresh water to make it to the camp, the next water stop.

There is a hierarchy to the visual signals of an overheating car. Model A's didn't have temperature gauges. The radiator cap was in plain sight; any steaming was sign enough of problems. The hierarchy ranged from lazy tendrils of steam (hot) to no visible steam coupled with a laboring engine emanating loud clanking noises (much too hot).

The last of our precious water was in the radiator and it was too hot to drive any farther. But this was an island. There was an oceanful of water surrounding us. It went against all my instincts to use salt water for cooling, but I figured there was plenty of it. It would cool the engine and could be flushed out with no lasting ill effects. I trudged the half mile across the dunes, waded out into the ocean, and scooped up a milk can full of ocean. The fog was still cotton wool thick. Walking in it was like walking in airy milk. By the time I returned, the car had cooled off, but the passengers were heating up.

"Are you sure we're going to be back by five, Eldridge?" they asked.

"We'll just drive along the ocean and dip in when we need to," I said. "Don't worry. We'll make it in plenty of time. No problem."

We kids had become experts at how to deal with overheated cars. The procedure was to start the hot engine and then pour in the cooling water to cool the blistering metal. It was quiet there in the foggy dunes. Very quiet. We listened to the starter grind over, and over, and over. It should have started right away. Something was awry. It was time to take a look under the hood. Probably whatever was wrong could be fixed in a jiffy. After all, this was a Model A.

Evidence of disaster has many guises. Some are minute. In this case a tiny, shiny, silvery drop of solder, about twice the size of a pinhead, shining brightly on the manifold was all I needed to see. I knew that car wasn't going to move for some time. That solitary, shiny drop of metal was a clear sign that the condenser had succumbed to the heat—its solder had melted. That condenser, smaller than half of my little finger, was a vital part of the car's primitive electrical system. Without it the Model A was as inert as a rock. I never carried a spare—nothing ever went wrong with condensers. It was the only time I ever heard of a condenser becoming liquid before or since.

It wasn't easy telling my bosses the predicament we were in, and they didn't make it easy. Their wives would be expecting them home soon, and we were facing an eight-mile walk in soft beach sand and they had no shoes. There was only the remotest hope that someone would come along. The only thing to do was to start walking north. We walked about a mile or so when I faced them with a decision: "Do you want to take a short cut that will save us a mile or so? It's cross country."

"We want to kill you Eldridge. If it wasn't so foggy we would. Be glad you are the only one that knows the way off this damn beach."

It seemed the glories of the beach had dissipated in the fog. After venting their spleens they decided the shorter way was the least onerous of the two choices. Up to this point their lack of shoes hadn't mattered much; we had been walking in the ruts, it was just warm, soft sand.

Striking off cross-country was quite different. The curses increased in volume and intensity, but again they had little choice but to follow and I, too, had little choice. At one point I turned to look at my sullen, mutinous group. Al was not far behind me. Bob was just visible in the tendrils of fog. Jerry was only audible, somewhere back there in the mists. From the volume and intensity of the imprecations coming from his direction, the visibilty must have been a little clearer in his vicinity. He was supposed to take his son to a baseball game at six and obviously wasn't going to make it.

We plodded on in the dense fog as darkness settled in around us, plodded through the small briers, the kind that catch and rake the tender skin between your toes. There were groans and more curses as we plowed through the sharp beach grass, more scratching and cutting, more curses, and more imprecations of doom. And when those tender feet were nicely lacerated, we found a wide area of poison ivy to wade through. They didn't notice this last hazard and I didn't think I'd point it out. They would find out in good time and I'd have time to leave the country. Alive. Maybe.

There is a quaintly named creek just south of Inward Point where the camps were, Hospital Creek. I also didn't think I'd tell the crew about this last obstacle until we encountered it. It's a great clamming creek at low tide; at high tide it is wide and deep. It was high tide and about five feet deep. Bob was five feet, five inches tall. When faced with this formidable crossing in the near dark, I thought the rough kidding about my premature demise was taking a more serious tone. The curses reached a crescendo at yet another level of vigor but again there was little choice. We had to slosh across the river or walk the mile or so around it. Three of us waded across on tiptoes; Bob had to swim. It's hard to curse while swimming, but somehow he managed, curses overlain with a little gurgling. I noticed too that, cursing or not, the gang was staying close. The closing darkness, combined with the dense fog, kept visibility to a just a few damp feet.

The camp with its hidden key tucked up under the eaves was a short distance from Hospital Creek. There, we found Band-Aids for the deepest cuts, old battered sneakers for some of the tender feet, a couple of dish towels to wrap around the others, and a can of cold beans for sustenance. Resuscitated and somewhat refortified, we began the long slog off the beach. We had five miles to go, but there was one slight chance that there might be someone to give us a ride. Just slightly off our straight line trek back to the boat was the Young's camp. Quite a gang used the place and used it at unpredictable intervals. There just might be someone there that could give us a ride off the beach. It was a slender chance but worth a try.

My glum band and I trudged through the soft sand and the thick fog until we could make out the dark bulk of the Young's camp, and like the star over the promised land we saw the feeble yellow glow of a kerosene lantern. Hallelujah! Someone was there, a ride off the beach was in the offing. I rapped on the door. What opened the door would have given pause to St. Peter. Tack was not a natty dresser in the best of circumstances. Out at the camp like most of us, his meager sartorial efforts were in eclipse. He hadn't shaved in three days and he was a little grungy around the edges, but his good-naturedness didn't desert him in the least when I asked for help.

"Tack, I'd never ask for myself, you know that, but I've got three hurting guys with me. We broke down by the lighthouse. Their wives were expecting them home around five. They're tired, they're worried, and they're about to kill me. Can you help us out?"

Tack rose to the challenge and quickly replied, "Sure, pile in the car and we'll take 'em off."

Sweet words, such sweet words. Salvation was at hand. This helpful soul acted as if he had been waiting for the call to help, as if being bothered at nine o'clock at night on an all but deserted island and asked to drive three strangers off the beach was what he had been hoping for.

I don't know what the original design mode of Tack's vehicle was except that its ancestry included a Model A. Whether it started its life as a pickup truck, a sedan, or a delivery wagon was lost in the mists of time. In its present guise it resembled a cross between a truck and a roadside cabin. What cab there was had been shingled. There was no hood, no fenders, no lights, no brakes, and the exposed radiator was connected to the cab by a drooping wire. The truck bed of this vehicle was ragged bits of plywood nailed to something below. It didn't exactly inspire confidence but it ran and as such, was infinitely better than anything I had. The lack of appurtenances were a trifling detail.

Tack was known as a goodhearted soul and certainly proved it that night.

He turned on the gas and stuck the crank in the front of the engine. He then had me pry up the engine (as with a lot of Model A's, the motor mounts were tired) to line up the crank hole with the engine, gave it a twirl or two, and the engine roared to life.

The Model A's gas tank was just in back of the rudimentary dashboard. Part of this car's delightful simplicity was the gravity feed gas flow; there was no balky fuel pump to break down. But having the gas tank in your lap didn't induce languor. The floorboards had long since gone the way of most of the rest of this traveling collection of odd parts. There was also no exhaust pipe. The yellow-blue flame of the exhaust came directly out of the manifold, right between the passengers' legs. For a short person, it would have been emasculation by immolation. In the still dense fog and the black night, this pulsating tongue of yellow-blue flame was spectacular and blinding, and the loud staccato, deafening.

We headed up the beach with my three bosses in the back clinging to whatever would keep them aboard, myself in the passenger's seat straddling the blue flame. We could see not a thing. Black fog equals a black night and this night's fog was just a shade shy of rain. And as our chariot had no windshield we were soon nicely anointed with Monomoy dew.

As we cautiously fumbled our way north, Al gave me a tap on the shoulder and pointed to the foot-long tongue of pulsating yellow-blue flame. I just smiled and looked ahead at nothing. Al hit me harder and again pointed to the flame. I looked a little closer and saw what he was pointing at. Gas was leaking out of the tank's sediment bowl and steadily dripping right through the only light in sight, that tongue of flame. I yelled at Tack over the deafening engine cacophony and pointed to the potential explosion. He just shrugged, smiled, and we kept lurching along, leaking gas and belching flame.

At that time Monomoy's mid-section was a featureless shelf of white sand that, on the highest of tides, washed over. This washing over wiped out any tracks and on this night, that is what had happened. On a normal non-foggy night this didn't matter; the lights of town gave us a bearing. On this black fog night there were no bearings, no visibility, and no tracks at all. But as we had no lights, we couldn't have seen the tracks anyway. Tack somehow knew to head north and head north he did.

His car, like mine, had overheating problems and in no time at all the familiar symptoms were obvious. An arrow-straight rod of white steam from the capless radiator was spouting skyward to join the fog, much like a steam locomotive's obvious signature. The old car was starting to groan, the exhaust was now all yellow, and the motor was clattering louder than ever. Time for a watering. Tack had no compulsions about using salt water. He waded into the surf, scooped up a bucket of water, and poured it in. We zigzagged off the beach. We blundered from ocean to bay, steaming, roaring, gas dripping, and grateful. The old car or Tack must have had a homing instinct. Nothing else could explain how he found his way off that featureless beach in that black fog. It wasn't long before we were headed down Coast Guard Hill to the parking area across from Horne's.

We thanked Tack vociferously for his kind errand of mercy and listened to his assemblage of car parts clattering, clanging, and steaming as they disappeared into the fog back down the beach. His good nature and kindness were swallowed, but not dimmed, by that wall of opaque.

The erratic trip off the beach had broken the back of the incipient mutiny. It was now around ten and rather than wanting to kill me, they just wanted to get home to assuage their worried families. Their curses were muffled, their energy sapped. It was a silent row across the harbor; there were a few quiet mutterings like a distant surf, but mostly it was the tired silence that follows any ordeal.

The police and the families were all waiting when we rowed out of the fog. It was explanation time.

Forty three years later when I ran into Al at a hardware store, his first comment was, "Hey Eldridge, do you remember that night on Monomoy?"

It was "no problem".

Pete

Monomoy was (and is) a major shellfish producer. Clams, quahogs, and occasionally sea clams littered the flats which, in turn, supported a crew of diggers. Every low tide saw an army of hunched-over forms plucking the prized soft-shell clams out of their beds. But quahogs also lived on the fringing shoals and occasionally nature herself digs these animals out of the bottom; all we had to do was pick them up.

The cold hand of winter occasionally clamps its icy grip on the Cape with viselike force. During the coldest winters, the saltwater bays and inlets freeze solidly, changing the face of our land considerably. This face-changing can be followed by opportunity. One late winter's day, just after ice out, Monomoy's low course tide bared an uncommonly large area of the Common Flat, a multi-hundred-acre shoal ground just west of Inward Point in Nantucket Sound. It was separated from the island by a slightly deeper moat.

Pete Hartley was a fellow lover of all things to do with Monomoy. He was also a close and good friend and the closest thing to a brother I ever had. He and I were out prospecting on the rarely exposed Common Flat and stumbled on a bonanza. The great cakes of ice that had resided on the flats for the past few weeks had caused thousands of quahogs to wash out. The water swirling around the ice floes had apparently scoured away the sand beneath, and voila, there for the taking were legions of shellfish. A quahog bonanza that had dollar signs dancing all around that windswept flat.

The ideal way to transport these shellfish off the beach would have been by boat, but our boat was five miles from this fecund flat—and that boat was a rowboat. Five miles is a tedious row, to say nothing of a five-mile row back, heavily loaded. We had come down the beach in Pete's old, much loved, Model A beach buggy. Going out to the flat with the car was a cinch. The moat was only six inches deep and the old car could easily handle twice that depth.

This vehicle was well used to salt water immersions. Indeed, it had been totally submerged twice, resurrected, and was still in fine shape. That's a figure of speech; what it meant was the car still ran. There wasn't much left of the body. That had long since gone the way of all steel pickled in salt water and marinated in salt fog.

We scurried around picking up the quahogs until we had all the old car could carry. It was time to head for the fish market.

Our greed had been blinding. In our haste to garner the shellfish, we had paid little attention to the rising tide. Where the majority of the quahogs lay was the highest part of the flat, still nice and dry. But over where we had to ford the moat, the flooding tide had made the crossing too deep for even the long-legged, redoubtable Model A.

Model 'A's are remarkable cars, but that didn't mean we could teach it to swim. And if we couldn't teach it to swim, the rising tide was going to immerse it once again and we were going to be faced with a long, cold, five-mile walk off the beach in boots. No small endeavour.

Everything about the old car's motor was well adapted to deep water driving except the updraft carburetor. This vital part metered the gas and was mounted low on the side of the engine. Immersion greater than about a foot or so meant the engine was ingesting salt water, something Henry Ford hadn't planned on when designing this most versatile car.

Inspiration is often a handmaiden of desperation, and we were desperate. The moat was about 100 feet across. If we couldn't teach the old car to swim, maybe we could adapt it to snorkel.

First, we removed the fan belt; we didn't want the cooling fan throwing salt water all over the primitive wiring. Then, we disconnected the top radiator hose, jury-rigged it to the mouth of the carburetor, and tied it in an upright position with a piece of fish line. This gave the car eight or ten more inches of freeboard. (Is it called freeboard in a car?) Maybe that would be enough to ford the deepening stream, maybe not.

If it failed, the car with its load of quahogs was bound to go under anyway. If we made it, the short trip across the moat wouldn't overheat the engine to any serious degree. Once across, we could return the double duty hose to its rightful place, replace the fan belt, and fill her (all our cars were "her") up with salt water and head off the beach.

The results were anti-climatic and only slightly nerve racking. Into the water we went at the slowest speed possible to minimize wave action. We crept across the swirling tidal river with the exhaust bubbling up from the depths.

The old car never missed a beat, but its square radiator created a massive bow wave in the crossing. She plowed her way across the sea bottom like some giant mechanical horseshoe crab belching bubbles. With water pouring from every crevice, the redoubtable old car came up on the dry shore as if coming out of the water to survey its surroundings and perhaps lay some eggs. It was a simple matter to reconnect the radiator hose, replace the fan belt, dump in some of that previously threatening salt water, and head off the beach to the fish market.

The relief we felt when that car wallowed out of the water was immense. The car was safe and the quahogs were headed to market. The relief gave way to giddy laughter as the realization set in that the improbable snorkeling had done the job. We were to be spared that long walk home. How could you not love a car that worked so improbably so often and so well?

On each of the next two days we made low tide quahog trips before the low course tides ended and the moat became impossibly deep. A brief winter bonanza on what we had thought was a sterile flat.

Pete was a bit older but not so much that it mattered. We fought over the same girls and shared many adventures together on the island. He was as solid a man as I've ever known, sometimes wildly impractical but always fun. Until his premature death, he was family. Pete, like all of us, underwent some kind of soul-satisfying metamorphosis when he set foot on that magnificent beach.

Pete wrote the following in the old *Cape Cod Standard Times*. This article appeared on January 6, 1974, and told of his earlier times on Monomoy:

> One of the things you don't do if you are a beginning teacher
> in a small New England town is go around setting smoky,

greasy fires on the beach. As far as I know no one in Chatham to this date knows that it was Dana Eldridge and I who were responsible for the congregation viewing a conflagration. They were fire officials, police and Coast Guard gathered at Chatham Light on a slightly hazy, early September afternoon.

They were trying to figure what was causing the pall of dense black smoke that was rising and blowing to the northeast five or six miles down Monomoy. Was it a boat ashore? Was some camp going up? Was it a grass fire?

It was none of these. It was a pile of junk and tires—about twenty of them, heaped on the tattered remains of a 1938 Ford station wagon that had once belonged to one of the Robie boys, but for the last six months had been sitting on the beach, stripped and an eyesore.

In a way it was an ecological gesture on our part, an attempt to beautify the beach and clean out the dump at the camp. The camp had been a project that we'd been working on at that time for about three years.

I'd met Dana when he began resurrecting an old gunning camp at Inward Point that belonged to his uncle. I insinuated myself into the deal, with the result for the next six or seven years I had a place to live on the beach. Putting the camp back together was a long involved, and sometimes ingenious process that in actual cash outlay came to something less than five dollars, until the spring I bought a gallon of paint and painted the floor.

Everything else, including furnishings, came from abandoned camps, the old World War ll aerial bombing target (the bulls-eye of which was a large flat, wooden cone built of nice tongue and grooved pine), from friends, and from the dump.

Even the shingles were used. Just turned around to their good side and nailed on.

The tool shed was an old duck hunter's sink box which we found in beautiful shape up in back of what was known as Brant Island until it washed away. We set it on end, slapped a door on, extended the overhang on the roof over it and voila, a tool shed!

When the project began, though, the first problems were perhaps the hardest. The camp was tiny, a box no more than

8 feet by 10 feet with a gable roof, and it was over on its side in the most dense growth of poison ivy I've ever seen. The windows and door were out of it, but a small faded sign over the door-hole announced 'Poison Ivy Camp.'

With a system of levers and bull strength, we righted the building, set it on blocks and went to work. Half our time was spent scrounging for materials, the other half in actual building.

We doubled the size of the main room, added a lean-to bunk-space (hardly large enough to be called a room), shingled the roof with asphalt shingles from at least four different sources and of four different colors, installed a warped black iron cookstove, slapped up some flue liner for a chimney, and we had a roof over our heads. Later came refinements, always with adventures.

There was the Sunday afternoon, for instance, when I was putting a window in and Dana had a date with him, a gorgeous red-haired nurse from Newton.

He wanted to show her the rest of the beach, so he took off with the word that if he wasn't back by four I was to come down the outside beach and hunt for him. What he forgot, of course, was that I didn't have a watch, he didn't have a watch and the camp didn't have a clock.

So off he went in his 1938 Chevy two-door down the beach with the red head, and back to my crude efforts at carpentry went I.

Four o'clock came and went, and when I finally came to the realization that he should have been back by now it was probably more like 5:30.

I cranked up my Model A station wagon and went charging off down the beach. Sure enough, there were Dana and the gorgeous redhead huddled behind some wreckage about opposite Monomoy Lighthouse in front of a small fire. Dana had a large welt on his head.

He'd gone sailing over the edge of a sand dune and wound up at the bottom of a perfect bowl, 40 feet deep and maybe 100 or 150 feet in diameter with both back springs on the Chevy busted and a first lesson in flying behind him.

The next week, it was only by jacking the Chevy off its

axle, blocking the frame away from the axle and wiring the whole thing together that he could begin any rescue attempt on the car.

Then by a series of gradually lengthening backward and forward leaps with the car, he worked it up over the edge of the sandy bowl. When the ultimate leap came, it meant another ferocious lump on the head, but the car made it. I never saw the redhead again, however.

There was the Thanksgiving vacation when I hitchhiked down from Connecticut with a friend and the three of us shingled in the snow and consumed three and half quarts of fresh quahog chowder at one sitting.

There was the hot July day that I found the foredeck of some long vanished fishing boat up in the marsh at Hammond's Bend and practically lost the Model A in what seem to be a bottomless pit of black mud trying to recover it. I got out with lots of help, and the deck made a great front porch.

A three-legged tower-platform-flagpole got built, essentially to provide a use for the flight of stairs we found on the beach.

And ultimately the outhouse from the old Monomoy Coast Guard Station got transported to its own little valley down beyond the tower.

All the while, building scraps that wouldn't go in the stove, bits and pieces of the continual parade of old automobiles that served us, and above all tired tires, were piling up in the area we designated as our dump across the road from the camp deep in the bayberry bushes.

By the fall of 1957 it was becoming unsightly. And by that time, too, both of us had married, and our lives were a little more settled and civilized.

He was at U Mass that year, and I had just come back from a summer in southern Ohio, where my son had been born in August, to take up my first teaching job at Chatham High School.

There was a hazy southwest wind blowing that September afternoon when we devised the plan to clean the dump and get rid of the unsightly wreck on the beach all in one fell swoop.

We loaded our cars with everything they could hold, drove out to the outside beach and heaped the wreck high with tires, old generators and starters, parts of wooden station wagon bodies, boxes, paint cans—everything we could transport, splashed a gallon or so of gas on the pile, fired her off and took off down the beach to the southard, fishing.

With nothing within a hundred yards that could catch fire and an offshore wind anyhow, we hadn't a worry in the world that our clean-up-the-beach campaign could give anybody at all any grief.

Later, by accident I heard abut the gathering of concerned officials at Chatham Light that afternoon, but I never said anything, and if anybody did know, they obviously didn't tell the school committee, or my teaching career would have been over almost before it began.

The camp was still there the last time I was at Inward Point. The key was still hanging on the same rusty nail under the eaves in the same place.

I went in and looked around at the battered stove, and the same oil lamps with the cracked chimneys, and the same smell, and the same notation on the back of the door to the food cabinet: 'D. Eldridge, T. Logan, P. Hartley consumed 3 1/2 qts. quahog chowder, 11/24/55.'

If I could capture one moment of my life, I'd be standing in the door of the camp on a quiet early autumn night with the smell of woodsmoke in the air, and soft lamp light behind me, and something bubbling heartily on the stove.

Away off to the north I'd hear the laboring chatter of a Model A Ford without a muffler grinding down the beach. There'd be the muffled mutter of low surf on the back shore, and for a moment, the stars would be very, very close.

We shared some wonderful times, times that have lasted in memory. Pete had a large heart and unfortunately, a short life. I miss his wry humor. I miss Pete.

Bookmarks of the Mind

I'm sure there is a psychological reason for the increasing clarity of the common sights we once took for granted, sights such as the green painted peanut butter jar we kept the matches in and the mouse-gnawed candles after a long spell away from the camp. Or the soft flickering, yellow light of the kerosene lanterns, especially when seen on a fog-shrouded evening—all the "little things" like precious relics on a shelf of thought. The bookmarks of the mind.

Not all the "little things" took place in the camp. One late summer evening we were out on the Common Flat just wandering around as the sun set over Nantucket Sound in its usual glorious display. The unusually low tide exposed areas of the flat that were rarely dry. We thought we would explore these previously unexplored sands. There were almost always treasures to be found and occasionally these treasures would be lucrative as well. It was a good search, no quahogs, no clams, no scallops, but we had a slow walk on a calm warm evening accompanied by the slowly setting sun. It was a lovely evening, warm with the Cape's usual soft southwest breeze. The rising tide started sliding up over the damp sand, gently shooing us back to shore, emphasizing the juxtaposition of natural wonders, the tide coming and the light going. In the half light of the fading day we began to notice little gray triangles sticking out of the water. They were towing widening v-shaped ripples silently through the water. These triangles were about four inches on a side and as we watched, they became more numerous, one about every ten square yards for as far as we could see. The water deepened, the day darkened, and the triangles moved closer. Suddenly they evolved into hundreds of little sand sharks coming in with the tide in the dying light of the sun; they, too, wanted to garner whatever the rising tide revealed.

They, too, were looking for the treasures of the tideland, but for a more fundamental purpose. It was a wonderful sight. We stood transfixed by yet another example of nature's abundance.

Only once since that time have we had the privilege of seeing these ancient fish in such numbers. It was during a slow, greasy calm trip back from Nantucket. My wife, Lynne, and I saw thousands of spiny dogfish showing their characteristic triangular dorsal fins and traveling in small groups of two or three. These fish too, were in all directions as far as the eye could see.

Another unusual happening occurred on the bay side of Inward Point. My father and I were walking along the tide line, coming back from a unique experience. On a wood collecting trip I had with unerring precision managed to get two flat tires simultaneously. We had only one spare. It was early evening, there was still plenty of light, and we were trudging back to the camp in an inch or two of Nantucket Sound's warm water. Somehow, I managed to step on a seaweed covered, nail-studded board, and one of those nails punched through the toughest part of my calloused foot. I rarely wore shoes anywhere if I didn't have to, and I never wore them on Monomoy. It was only with Wib standing on the board and both of us pulling, that my foot was unpinned. The minor exertion opened a little hole that bled a trickle.

We encountered a sea robin (an odd-looking but usually innocuous fish) that apparently had a carnivorous bent. Either that or he was extremely proprietary. In the inch or two of warm water appeared this pugnacious ten-inch fighter or biter. This minute bit of fishdom harried us all along the shoreline for at least a quarter of a mile. If we so much as splashed the water he was there ready to do battle. I wanted to rinse out the nail hole by walking along in the warm salt water. He didn't want me in "his" water. Why, we couldn't imagine. The thought did occur to us that maybe my bleeding a little had something to do with his single-minded attention to me; he, if it was a he, didn't pay any attention to Wib. This pugnacious fish all but stranded himself numerous times in his attempts to drive us out of his domain and maybe, off "his" beach. We chuckled at the antics of this fishy David for all the long walk back. He gave up the chase only when we turned inland to the camp. I like to imagine that as he watched us walk away, he thought he had triumphed and gave himself a congratulatory pat on the back. Perhaps too, there was a Mrs. Sea Robin lurking in the deeper water cheering her hero on. We felt a little like cheering him on ourselves.

The "little things" of those years come unbidden as vignettes pleasantly engraved on the mind to be examined from time to time with a smile in the recalling.

The Ocean's Maw

But the smiles were for the memories. For the camp itself, the end was near. The Atlantic's advance was not to be deterred. Each savaging northeast wind moved a little more sand away than the westerlies replaced. As the camp's fortunes were wending toward a wet finality, I acquired a family and the camp was no longer the focus of my life. The demands of family life limited our use of this building, though not entirely. As in the generations before, financial limitations decreed that the camp, the boats, and the cars take a back seat to the demands for college, dental care, doctor's visits, and Little League, all the essential details. But as time and finances permitted, we did use the little building.

All three of the boys (we had no girls) have camp memories. On at least half a dozen occasions, we all spent the night there—nights when we went fishing the dawn over on the bar and nights when I just wanted them to experience waking up in that snug little haven. They are the last generation of Eldridges who will have memories of stirring to consciousness with the sun streaming in the camp's windows or seeing that magnificent orb rising majestically out of the blueing ocean over Schooner Bar. They will remember the noisy and sometimes smoky stove-lighting ritual, the stove that consumed so much driftwood, heated the camp so often, and produced so many delicious meals. Those experiences are in their memory banks, stored away in the part labeled "Open for pure pleasure anytime." The boys have had the merest glimpse through a window of time, a glimpse that is now curtained forever. The three boys, all of us here on this mobile peninsula, know that sooner or later, all of the Cape's buildings will follow the land, lemming-like, into the ocean. Cape Cod is made of sand. The ocean is rising at an increasing rate. The end, when it comes, is never a surprise. But hurt, oh Lord, does it hurt. Much like the final absence of an old friend, the ache of the loss never really leaves. It subsides, it retreats, but it is always there.

All the generations to follow will never know how free and unfettered life on the Cape had been. How the sense of belonging, being part of the Cape, came to life in the low-tech world that was our camp and our beach. It was a world where ingenuity meant more than education, where hard work produced immediate and tangible results, a place where we lived on a masterpiece of nature's design and took it all for granted. Until we couldn't anymore.

The ocean isn't a bit fussy when it takes happiness. It can sneak in the dark of night or it can come with all the grace of the wrecker's ball to do its dirty work.

My parents' camp was on the inside beach. Here, the ocean succeeded in a stealthy approach—no roaring surf, no dramatic smashing blow, just oceanic stealth.

One black, late spring night, a tide higher than any before or since slithered cold, dark, and silent into the camp's little hollow in the dunes. It must have sinuously coiled around and over the fireplace's hearth—the one we had built with such laughter, the scene of so many driftwood fires.

Next, the frigid waters must have inundated the firebox of that marvelous old Glenwood stove, cooling it forever. The magnificent old stove that had cooked so many delicious meals, that had warmed the camp so many times, was in the final embrace of a force far greater than man's.

Probably about the time the firebox was being submerged, the chairs were beginning to float uneasily around the place, moved for the first time in their existence by something other than human hands. In their unguided motion, they must have bumped into what had been the stacked firewood that had filled the fireplace—firewood that had been placed indoors to stay dry for the next trip we made down to the camp.

Also about this time the two lower bunks would have felt the chill waters soaking the mattresses and the blankets. Then, as the waters advanced to the second tier of bunks, it would have been the pillows' turn to feel the black water's embrace.

As the waters continued their inexorable rise, the table and couch would have joined the soggy assemblage of suddenly dreary objects in a sodden, slow-motion dance, curtsying and bowing as the dark waters came in through the multitude of cracks and crevices and all but filled the old place.

Then the tide ebbed and apparently ebbed fast.

When we saw what had been the wellspring of so much joy, the roof was sitting on the floor and the four walls were splayed out in the four compass directions. It looked as though the tide had eased in and gone out in a rush.

The camp hadn't floated, it had exploded with the weight of the water inside of it, water that couldn't get out quickly enough. If only we had thought to put in scuppers, it would probably still be standing. Of the three camps we owned on the island, it is the only site still out of the ocean's maw.

The ocean, though, cared little for good times or bad, and it had a different, more dramatic treatment in store for my uncle's camp, the camp I called mine. When the Outer Beach was breached, this little building was surely in harm's way. The breach widened and took first the Young's camp, then Daisy's camp next door, and then a year after the cut-through, it was my small bit of heaven that had to go through the all but choreographed dance. First it was buried by the advancing dune, then as the dune moved inland the little building was fully exposed to the ocean's might. The old recycled henhouse, the much beloved little camp, and the advancing ocean met one stormy winter day. The implacable ocean was not in any sense polite when it announced its arrival. It didn't knock gently at the door, it knocked mightily at the closest wall, and the camp was gone as though it never was. For a brief period there were shingles, window sashes, and broken boards littered along the surf-line heading south toward Nantucket and Long Island. Lovely litter.

I miss it, but it isn't only the camp that is missing and causing that nagging ache in my heart. I was able to salvage an old ship's knee we had picked up many years before. This knee, once a vital part of a sailing vessel, had been a corner bookshelf and a candle holder. This angled piece of wax-bespattered, worm-eaten wood can bring back the idyllic memories with just a glance. It is my Monomoy talisman.

Life is nothing if not a succession of changes. We have to deal with them. It only remains for us to choose how are we going to handle these changes. Positively or negatively, it's our choice. Our childhood Eden had gone the way of the Cape Cod heath hen. It was like a film, but there would be no reruns. It was time to move on, to find another Shangri-La. We cannot capture that which is gone.

But we can reminisce about the delightful times and open our eyes to the new opportunities that surround us all.

While not letting go of that rich and rewarding past, we can reach to embrace the always uncertain future.

Part IV
Warren Baker, Raconteur

The Cape Codder Newspaper

No matter what *The Cape Codder* reported, the old, the new, the soon to be, the paper always kept its eye on what the Cape was all about.

Every issue had a tide table. These tide tables didn't stop the Cape's northeasters. In January of 1952, the paper covered a severe storm that slammed into the Cape. The Orlean's basketball team was on Nantucket for a game, and there they stayed for five days until the ferries could resume service. Just a month later, another nor'easter came smashing into the Cape's bended arm, and this storm had as much snow as most of us had ever seen on the Cape. The rotary near the Hyannis Airport was plowed one lane wide. The snow was well over the road signs. Giant rotary plows from Maine were brought in to clear the roads.

During this same storm, in the heaving waters off Chatham's east flank, a rescue occurred that is still being talked about.

The Coast Guard had received word that a tanker was in trouble off Boston. The garbled message indicated the ship had broken in half. A plane was sent out to check out the situation and it did find a tanker bow floating around well off Provincetown. The best the pilot could make out on this fragment was a name, Fort Mercer. Not far away, the stern half soggily rode the huge waves and this half had men aboard. The pilot had done his job in nearly impossible circumstances. He had found the wreck so help could be given. As he was heading back to base, his mission accomplished, he could scarcely credit his senses when out of the spume and spindrift he saw yet another stern half of an identical tanker. Two tankers had broken in half within a dozen miles of each other on the same night. The second tanker, the Pendleton, eventually came to rest just off Monomoy's east shore, where it became a rusting monument to the fury of a roused ocean. But not before thirty-two of the thirty-three men aboard were plucked from a sure watery death by three courageous young Coast Guardsmen who risked all.

Not one of the commercial fishermen who watched the tiny U.S.C.G. thirty-six-footer butt its way into those massive, storm-driven waves, ever expected it to return. Later revelations by the crew of the small boat revealed that they, too, didn't really expect to return.

Until that night, the Coast Guard's reputation was spotty at best. Ever after, their reputation, at least in Chatham, has had a sterling luster.

By 1952 the Outer Cape was growing up. It had cast its lot with sensible growth as evidenced by the passage of Senator Stone's bill authorizing the two-year community college. Towns were adopting zoning, albeit after much wrangling at the often boisterous town meetings.

The ever-increasing hordes of vacationers were wearing out our pitiful oiled roads. A bill to pave the roads in Nickerson State Park was passed. But road improvements all over the Cape brought their own problems.

The free and easy ways of the past were slipping into memory as more and more people came to call. It was a juxtaposition of feelings. We all saw the advantages the newcomers were bringing—the good restaurants, a better hospital, improved schools, all the positive things that make an area extra special. But in the wake of the increasing numbers came increasing restrictions and limits. Indeed, the area was changing before our eyes and changing into something only similar to what we had grown up with. Permits, something we had never heard of before, were now necessary for fires or gatherings on the beach. The new rules made hurtful sense.

Common sense decreed that rules had to be applied, but for those of us who had known the unrestricted past, it chafed a bit to be limited in an environment that we thought limitless. And although most of us didn't realize it at the time, we, too, were being educated in the limitations large numbers of newcomers brought along. There even seemed to be some ambiguity among the newcomers. They wanted to know and see the "old Cape," but only if it didn't infringe on their comfort or peace of mind.

Along with the increasingly restrictive limits, the traditional conflicts reassured us that all of the old Cape wasn't going the way of the Cape's extinct heath hen.

A 1953 Cape Codder headline read, " 'Scallop War' Between Chatham and Orleans Threatened as Chatham Charges Line Pushed South—Resurvey Held." Now here was something we could find familiar, something we could get our teeth into—fighting over a bountiful scallop crop. It's a battle that stirs Cape Codders just as much today and in much the same fashion. If one town has a scallop bonanza, naturally the adjoining town is going to want to share in the treasure. Disputes over the exact placement of a boundary can mean the difference between going to court or going home with a nice bucketful of those delectable scallop eyes. And even if you knew you were just over the line in forbidden waters, maybe you could convince the warden that a little fog blurred the line enough to claim ignorance or innocence.

Blue Crabs

Our heaven, our haven, the little camp on Monomoy was gone and the new landlords of the island, the Fish and Wildlife Service, decreed that there would be no rebuilding. Their long-term goal was no human habitation on the island, just nature's creatures enjoying a human-free existence on Monomoy's varied environment. This was a laudable goal, one we could all understand, but one that hurt deep in our psyche. I agree with the overall aim of the Service, with our increasing numbers it is inevitable, but I surely miss that part of my heritage.

Missing the past had to be supplanted by exploring the future. This seems to be the way life is. We move on from the past and reach out to the undiscovered future to whatever is around the next corner. We find new delights just waiting to be explored.

As a child I spent my summers in a cabin overlooking a small tidal creek off Nantucket Sound in South Chatham. Nearly every summer we spent some time blue crabbing at night with a bright flashlight. Not only was the hunt fun and often exciting, but the eating was the best. Few treats from the sea have the exquisite taste of the blue crabs. They are at least one order of magnitude better than lobster.

Cape Cod is at the extreme northern limit of blue crab habitat. As far as I know, they have never occurred in Cape Cod Bay and despite the name, Pleasant Bay, these fast-moving crustaceans only occasionally occur in the Bay's inviting waters. But they are eagerly awaited and when they do "strike in," they bring pleasure with them—gustatorial pleasure written in boldface.

This book has been almost single-mindedly about Monomoy. But blue crabs, one of the stellar treats Cape Cod has to offer, are rarely if ever found on Monomoy, and we love blue crabs. The sheltered waters, the marsh creeks they so desire, are all but absent on that sandy peninsula.

When, by a fluke of circumstance, they deign to appear along the south shore of the Cape, we know extra-good eating is in the offing—eating that to a lot of us exceeds lobster in flavor. And not only is the extra-good eating a reward, the catching is a fun exercise as well.

It's a catching that somehow seems right (at least to us—the crabs might have a different point of view). Most of these crabs will not survive our cold winters; they are doomed anyway. Like the delicious bay scallop, adulthood is the end of the line for them. We, by eating them, are merely moving up the inevitable. We are not reducing a resource.

The sleek, beautiful blue crab is strictly a creature of summer. They don't like cold weather any better than most of us. Come winter they die out or hide out.

But summertime's warm waters are an invitation to the crabs to move about, and also a goad for us to unlimber the dip nets and get new batteries for the flashlight. An article I wrote in *The Cape Codder* in 1986 describes a crabbing expedition as we used to do them in the early days on Eel River in South Chatham:

Blue crabbing is a great way to spend a summer evening. Not only is it fun, but if successful, there is the very real prospect of a crab feast.

On a typical crabbing trip we push off from the dock in the golden glow of a yellow rose sunset, row and drift down the river to a likely spot to begin the crabbing expedition.

One mans the spotlight, another hops overboard to maneuver the boat and net the crabs. The water here is only a couple of feet deep.

Ideally one or two guests will be along to help out and share the evening. Most summer evenings on the Cape are cool, so a thermos of hot coffee will be appreciated later on.

The lightman usually flashes the light around, slicing away the darkness Excaliber like, blinding everyone temporarily. Then he settles down to do some serious crab spotting.

What we all look for is either the crab shape itself or a straight, white horizontal line. That line is either a razor clam shell or a crab facing you. The line is straight because crabs don't smile much (one we saw was eating a very dead eel, certainly not the stuff of smiles).

The netman pulls the boat along and the water in front of him is the blackest black. All manner of surprises await the netter's bare toes—spider crabs, blue crabs, horseshoe crabs (the ones the old-timers called "hossfoots"), rocks, holes, deep-clinging mud and drop-offs. It all sounds hazardous in the extreme but in many years of barefoot crabbing, I've only been nipped once.

At first, despite the incentive of a delicious crab meal, no one pays any attention to the crabs. The illumination of the underwater doings is mesmerizing and so different from what you would expect. Life is everywhere, darting, scuttling, zipping, out of the water, in the water. Silversides skitter, explode from the water with the caress of the light. Most of these smaller fish are on the very edge of the shallow waters, probably to evade the predatory snapper blues that patrol the deeper waters like aquatic wolves.

Gar fish, looking vaguely prehistoric, torpedo through the water, their long thin jaws armed with needle-like teeth. Very formidable predators. We are glad they don't grow any bigger.

Eels lurk everywhere, a head here, a tail there, usually under some grass or seaweed in their never-ending search for sustenance.

A couplet of hossfoots cruise by, seemingly oblivious to all, coming from man's prehistory. These aquatic spiders (they actually are cousins to the spiders) demand a certain respect; they have been around, unchanged, for a lot longer than man and they may well outlast us yet.

Over against the bank is an emerging midden heap, the dirt-stained shell fragments evidence of other early bay inhabitants, Native Americans. They also went crabbing just as we are. Our light is electric, theirs flame; our net is nylon, theirs wood and sinew. But the enthusiasm is the same, the anticipation is the same, and the blue crab is the same.

There, in the light is a crab, a keeper, ready to go either way. All tense now, the netter slowly and carefully advances the net. A quick swoop and the crab is caught, along with about a half a bucketful of seaweed, the whole dumped into the waiting bucket.

If you wait too long to dump the net, the crab wakes to the fact he is in trouble and thoroughly entangles himself. Then you are in for some fun. The crab is quite angry and has sharp claws, your fingers quite soft.

If perchance your scoop misses the bucket, the crab plops on the deck. Great excitement, knowing those fast-moving crustaceans with those sharp-biting claws are cruising around our soft bare toes in the dark—perks up the gathering no end.

But our light doesn't just light up the bottom. By the very reflective nature of water, some light is reflected back into the sky. When we pass under some overhanging trees, this reflection takes on a life of its own. Undulating striations of light pattern the overhanging leaves, a green kaleidoscope, another visual gift.

With any luck, an hour or two of gazing and crabbing will produce enough crabs for a meal. We take only the males. They seem to be bigger and are easily identified. They have the narrow belly strap, the females the broad rounded strap.

Everyone is tired, damp, a bit cold (time for that coffee), and surfeited with images to treasure. Once again Pleasant Bay has produced in abundance.

It's time to go. Leave some for the next time. Respect the system that produces so much.

Get ready to enjoy a heaping platterful of bright red, steaming (and still somewhat truculent looking) blue crabs that are sweeter than lobster.

As I mentioned earlier, blue crabs are not an always thing. Only about every six or eight years or so do they strike in. The scientists tell us it has something to do with the confluence of coastal currents and Delaware Bay blue crab spawning activity. Whatever the reason, the crabs do show up from time to time, and we are always ready.

A Passion for Life

Blue crabs are not only good to eat but, in this instance, serve as a nice introduction to an old and dear friend, Warren Baker.

Earlier in this book some of The *Cape Codder's* articles described Cape Cod characters that were mostly before my time. I had the immense good fortune to meet one of these sterling people whose life overlapped mine and those earlier times. Not only was he delightfully unconventional, but he had a passion for life that is seen in few. He was fun to know and a pleasure to be around. He was a true Cape Cod character, and for the last fifteen years of his life, I spent as much time with him as I could.

Born in Chatham, Warren spent most of his life in Orleans and retired to Brewster. One of the old Cape Cod Bakers, he was at least a generation and a half older than I but in one sense we were like brothers. I met him when he was in his mid-sixties and I in my mid-thirties. As far as I was concerned he was ageless. The thirty-year difference in our ages wasn't a factor in our relationship. He was interested in everything, game for anything, and had done just about everything Cape Codders can do. He provided for his family in a handsome way. His various business enterprises never faltered for lack of hard work or imagination. He and I once had a handshake transaction. It worked out that by breaking his word to me he would have gained at least $20,000. He didn't break his pledge. As he told me later when I confessed my nervousness about the transaction, "There was no need to worry, boy, we shook on it."

Physically he was a little rough-hewn around the edges. Mentally, he was very sharp. There was little about the Cape and its waters that Warren didn't know all about. He loved everything about the outdoors. He was at once a duck hunter and a duck lover. He was an ardent goose hunter who would go to great lengths to make nesting platforms for these big beautiful birds. He was involved in aquaculture twenty years before it became the business it is now.

Warren lived by his wits and his lively intelligence. He cushioned life with quick humor, and his many stories were the stuff of the Cape. There were many such stories over the years, some of which are repeated here. And some I can't relate are even better than these.

Warren belonged to a different time. He once told me how at age six he was playing with his brother in a field near his home in Chatham. A friend of theirs, another six-year-old, Josh, more smartly turned out than usual, went by. Josh was one of the prolific Cape Cod Nickersons who was to become a positive force in the growth of the Cape. He told Warren he was going to school, and wondered why Warren wasn't going, too. As Warren related the story, he had never heard of school. He ran back home and asked his mother if he too could go to school. She guessed he could, cleaned him up a bit, found some shoes that fit, and sent him off.

I felt I had met a kindred soul when I met Warren. He had heard about some work I was doing with shellfish aquaculture and was interested in the project. Nothing would do but he had to know more, and in his direct way, he came to our home and knocked on the front door. I opened the door on the beginning of a solid friendship that endured until his death.

I often think of his kindness and compassion for those he met along the way. He seemed to always see the human side of any situation and usually had a commonsense way of dealing with whatever came along. But mostly I admired his passion for life. Whatever he did, he did with gusto and verve. There aren't enough passionate people out there.

* * *

One fine spring day, Warren and I were down on the bay fishing for flounder. Warren was keeping smaller fish than I was. I queried him about it.

"How come you are keeping those small fish?" I asked. "They are the devil's own job to fillet."

I thought I was going to learn some new way to clean flatfish from this quintessential Cape Codder.

"Nothing to it boy. I just throw them in the sink. Helen (his usually very tolerant wife) cleans them."

That was great, but unfortunately for me, my grandmother (who until then had never shown any evidence of a mean streak) had at an early stage forewarned my new wife of the consequences of learning to clean fish. Warren did go on to say he had once overstepped himself in the fish cleaning department, that he was now a little more careful about what he said.

Warren, like any Cape Codder, was never one to pass up a meal from the bay's aquatic pantry. In his semi-retirement he ran a string of eel pots, which for him necessitated two trips a day roaming those bountiful, shallow waters he loved so much. Whenever the crabs struck in, Warren was one of the first to know and one of the first to take advantage of this culinary treat.

During one banner year of crab abundance, he brought home a nice mess of those scrappy pinchers.

" Helen, we're having a crab salad for supper," he announced.

If you have ever picked crabs you know what a tedious job it is. The meat is snow white and the shell separators that compartmentalize the meat are also snow white, snow white and brittle. It's almost impossible to keep bits of this shell out of the meats.

What Warren was doing was asking Helen to fix his crab for him, as he had asked many times before, and as I'm sure she had done many times before. But picking crabs is always a difficult and thankless task.

Warren came home that evening, and sure enough, the crab salad was waiting for him. This was the first time in years the crabs had been plentiful, and my old friend was really looking forward to this meal with eager anticipation. His first mouthful of the crisp lettuce laced with that delicately flavored, absolutely fresh crabmeat was all anyone could have asked, the bay's best. The second mouthful was a slightly different story. This time a sliver of shell wedged between his teeth and pricked his gums, enough to sting a bit but not enough to really bother him. He made a big production of extracting the offending shell, scowled across the table, and was careful to put the shell fragment on the side of the plate facing Helen. He wanted her to see the error of her ways. With the third mouthful, Warren's notably short temper reached its limit. Another shell fragment drove a little deeper into his gums, deep enough to draw a jewel-like drop of bright red blood. Again, he extricated the fragment with the utmost visible effort, grimacing all the while.

He held the shell bit in plain view, scowled across the table at his wife of thirty-two years, and said, "Well Helen, you didn't do much of a job cleaning these crabs."

Helen, well used to Warren's posturings, was stung to the quick. It had been hard work cleaning those crabs.

"Well Warren," she countered, "you better enjoy them because I did a darn sight better job on these crabs than I'll ever do again."

And that was Warren's last crab salad.

Taking a cue from my friend's experience, we serve crabs much differently. Everyone gets six or eight spread newspaper pages at their place, a small cup of drawn butter, nut crackers, and nut picks. The bright red, steamed crabs, mounded five or six high, come to the table on the old, white milkstone platter, with clouds of savory steam mushrooming up and across the ceiling. From that point on it's every man for himself. The juices fly as the shells are removed and the meat extricated. Catching these creatures is an adventure in itself. So, too, is the eating, getting the quarter pound or so of that delicious white meat out of the labyrinths of that brittle shell. Is it worth it? It sure is.

* * *

I sometimes wonder how the first people to try some of the foods we now eat with gusto ever figured out how to prepare them. The courage for sampling food is of a different order than the courage needed to gather food.

Courage is a trait shared by many, the quiet courage that keeps one going when the odds seem impossibly high. Warren told me of one of his sea scalloping trips up off Truro.

Cape Cod in March is cold, and if it's been a cold winter, the ice hasn't been long out of bays and ponds. In the really cold winters, Cape Cod Bay itself will freeze at least a mile or so from the nearest shore. When that happens the bay is frigid long into the spring.

Warren and a friend decided to go after some sea scallops one early March day, just after the ice retreated from the bay. They wanted to get a jump on the season and also get a little extra money after a long, lean winter. As is often the case, outfitting the boat and rigging the gear was a hurried, last-minute operation. But come March first, the opening day of the season, they were ready. Two days after the last of the ice left the bay, they launched the boat, rigged the drag, and were prepared for the first sea scalloping trip of the year. Sea scalloping, in this case, involved a thirty-five-foot boat, an eight-foot steel drag that weighed about 1,000 pounds empty, and two men. Then it was a matter of knowing where the scalloping grounds were, having the skills to work the equipment, and offering a fervent prayer that the gods would be smiling on their endeavors.

From the story he told me, they steamed up off Truro somewhere, lined up on their ranges, dropped the drag and made a tow.

The first few drags were exploratory and then they found the spot they were looking for. Every tow had a nice batch of scallops in it and all the equipment was working just fine. It looked like a lucrative day in the making. In their hurry to get all the gear together though, one of them had neglected to bind off the end of the wire rope that pulled the drag. That left a bird's nest of stiff, frayed, wire rope ends frizzing out like a cat's claws, ready to snag anything that came into its path. On about the fifth tow, the seat of Warren's oilskins came into its path and those frayed wire ends caught and held just as Warren released the winch to lower the heavy drag over the side for another tow. The drag, with Warren attached, went down like a stone, into that dark, frigid water.

The great weight of the drag took him down fast, so fast a considerable amount of air was trapped in his oilskins. When the drag slammed into the bottom, about thirty feet down, Warren knew he was a dead man, and except for that bubble of air in the oilskins he would have been right. The buoyancy in his clothes combined with the jar of the drag slamming into the bottom, ripped out the seat of his pants and released Warren, who promptly bobbed to the surface like a cork. Ah, saved, thought he, but alas it was not to be.

When he arrived at the surface there was no help in sight—only his own boat with his crewman at the wheel stolidly steaming away, totally oblivious to his captain in the water, just a short distance behind. Yelling wouldn't do any good; the unmuffled engine obliterated thought, to say nothing of speech, and by now the chill of that thirty-degree water was starting to intrude on the excitement of the occasion.

His thoughts must have been wildly cyclical. From the routine working of the drag to facing certain death seconds later, to apparent salvation when he ripped loose and bobbed to the surface, to facing a slower death when he realized his crewman didn't even know he was overboard. What a kaleidoscope of feelings.

About the time he had given up desperately trying to will the man at the wheel to turn around, he found fortune hadn't forsaken him quite yet. The trip line for the drag came slicing through the water right beside him. This trip line was manila, a fiber rope attached to both the boat and the drag. It hangs in a long loop and drags along behind the boat during the tow. As it came by, Warren grabbed it like life itself. Saved again, he thought. The added drag of Warren on the trip line slewed the boat enough to wake the crewman out of his reverie. When he turned to see what the problem was, he discovered his friend in desperate straits. Cold to the core, hanging on with sheer will power, Warren was beginning to lose consciousness.

With the boat stopped in the water, the struggle to hang on to the moving line was eased, but at the same time, he found he was having trouble moving his arms. He had been in the icy water at least fifteen minutes and had been exerting himself to the utmost just hanging on to the moving rope. His body was very cold and he knew he didn't have long to live.

The crewman pulled the boat alongside Warren, and again salvation was at hand, but with Warren unable to help himself there wasn't much the crewman could do.

They stayed that way for a few minutes, just looking at each other, the crewman dry, secure, and helpless, standing on the deck a foot or two above Warren's head. He couldn't begin to lift his friend's inert and sodden mass out of the water and over the gunwale—no man on earth could have lifted such a weight.

Warren, in the icy water, was all but numb and by now, unable to speak. He just lay there with that dry deck so close but unable to help himself. In telling the tale, Warren said the easiest thing in the world would have been to lay back in the water and give up. He had reached the stage of life just prior to death, when all you have ever known recedes into a thickening opaque fog, an oasis of seldom experienced self. He was in no pain and the thought of sinking back in that soft, black water was all but overpowering. The overriding concern of how his wife would ever be able to raise their two children without his income kept him hanging on.

The crewman then got his thoughts together, tied a loose loop of line around Warren's neck so he couldn't slip away, and tied that line off. He then winched in the drag, maneuvered Warren into it, and hoisted the whole lot above the deck. He pulled the trip line and dumped Warren sprawling, waterlogged, and inert on that oh, so welcome deck.

Warren's clothes were stripped off, wrung out, and put back on. The crewman rooted around in the tiny, cluttered cabin, found a bottle of rum, and gave Warren a generous belt of that fiery restorative. Warren was, like most fishermen, a tough old guy. With his semidry clothes on, down in the snug, warm cabin out of the wind, and with the snort of that gut-warming elixir working in his bloodstream, it wasn't long before the world looked as promising as ever.

After he told me this story, I asked him if the tide was high enough so they could clear the bar and return to Rock Harbor.

" Return to harbor," he exclaimed. "Hell no, I had another snort and we finished out the day. Got our limit too".

Quiet courage.

This same man with his same indomitable spirit set out to garner a few ducks from Pleasant Bay's bountiful marshes one early morning.

"Hey, you. That your boat?"

The barked accusation came out of the predawn darkness like a thunderbolt. Duck hunting often means early morning starts, very early morning starts. One frosty predawn morning, Warren was set to go out to one of the islands in the bay by "borrowing" a skiff.

"Borrowing" used to be a time-honored way of using whatever was available, no matter whose it was. You were expected to take good care of it and return it exactly as you found it, but otherwise it was accepted and tolerated that from time to time, things not nailed down would be "borrowed."

As he drove up to the Horseshoe in South Orleans he saw that another hunter had just tugged and dragged one of the heavy wooden skiffs down to the water's edge. Without missing a beat Warren jumped out of his truck and yelled rather belligerently:

"Hey, you, that your boat?"

"No, no, I'm sorry mister," said the borrower. "Just thought I'd borrow this one. I'll get one of the others. Sorry."

Warren told me it wasn't his skiff either, but the other guy was younger than he was and that probably the exercise of turning over another heavy wooden skiff and dragging it down to the water's edge would do him good.

Warren was such a pleasure to be with and he had stories that seemed to go on forever. He was a born raconteur. To my everlasting regret I didn't tape his recounting of times past.

He managed to be on Nauset Beach when, during the First World War, a German submarine was shelling a tug boat. He told of sitting up on Nauset Heights watching the show. At another time he and his father helped unload a small freighter that had slid up on the outer beach off Chatham. He talked of standing watch at the Old Harbor Lifesaving station in the early 1920s, counting over 100 sails scudding up and down the coast during the westerlies and seeing no sails at all during the occasional easterlies.

In the 1920s, when Warren served at the station, it was common practice for the local fishermen to sign on each winter. It was a good arrangement for both the Lifesaving Service and the fishermen. The service needed men experienced with the local waters and the fishermen needed the income during the off season. Winter was also the season when most maritime troubles occurred.

The Old Harbor Coast Guard Station that now resides on the beach in Provincetown, was built and spent most of its life on the outer beach off Chatham's east shore.

Warren related the following story to me.

Captain Kelly, a martinet and the keeper of the Old Harbor Station, had to leave the station for a few days. He summoned Warren:

"Mr. Baker, I'm putting you in charge of this station for the time I'll be gone. I expect it to be in top shape when I get back. Any questions?"

There were none, but while Warren appreciated the trust placed in him, he knew it put him in a hard spot. He would have to enforce discipline and live among the men while he did so. Not only that, he had to keep the standards up to Captain Kelly's level of deportment, a standard far above what most of the men deemed necessary. One of these exacting rules was that there was to be no smoking while on lookout duty.

This seemed ridiculous to the watchkeepers, and with Warren's tacit approval the lookouts smoked during the captain's absence.

After the first few days' jitters, Warren managed the tightrope act of discipline and friendship with his usual good spirits. All the men knew the ticklish position he was in and helped out keeping the station shipshape.

On the day before the good captain was due back, any thoughts Warren might have had about the men's backing him were resolved when the boathouse roof caught fire. The watchkeeper's cigarette had rolled down the roof and ignited the tinder dry material in the gutter. The fire got a pretty good start before it was noticed, enough of a start that two or three boards burned through. Now, here was clear evidence of the rules being relaxed. Could it be fixed before the Captain returned the next day?

All hands turned to, and the charred shingles were ripped off and buried, the scotched boards removed and replaced, and new spare shingles applied. From the outside there was no evidence of the little conflagration. Inside, it was another story. Way up in a dark corner, a sharp-eyed observer could pick out the bright new boards. The men had forgotten to darken them to match the others and now there wasn't time to do it.

Warren knew his job depended on making sure Captain Kelly didn't see the repair job. If he did, the jig was up and Warren would be jobless.

Warren told me he did everything in his power to keep the captain's eyes on a downward slant; he pointed out how carefully the floors were swept, how well the men had cleaned and blackened the stove. In general and in particular the station was in excellent shape.

Warren was just starting to breathe a little easier when the captain requested they inspect the boathouse. Here, too, was a well-swept floor, the breeches buoy apparatus in meticulous condition. All was well and once again Warren was beginning to think that maybe they would get away with it. Such was not to be. At the last possible moment the captain's eyes swept up and right away he noticed the newness of the replaced boards. Warren's heart sank.

"Well, Mr. Baker, what's that?" he snapped, pointing to the evidence of the fire.

Warren told me he had one arrow left in his quiver.

"Well, Captain, that looks like the roof of the boathouse to me."

His gimlet-eyed chief surveyed the situation and after a long pause replied, "So it is, Mr. Baker, so it is."

Warren's quick wit (and the savvy captain's) saved his job.

***

In the interval between the two World Wars Warren turned his hand at whatever would turn a profit.

Prohibition became the law of the land in the early 1920s. The few years it lasted was a time of depravation for many and a time of opportunity for some few enterprising souls here on the Cape. Nearly every beach had a semi-buried bunker, a storage depot, lurking in some remote area along its length. Late night beach walkers grew accustomed to quiet waterborne activities, the rumble of powerful engines, the quick, quiet shuttling of cargo from boat to bunker. Any such commotion was a clear signal to any observers to walk the other way. Occasionally the shoreside dwellers would be treated to an audible show—roaring boat engines, yells, occasional shots, then all would be quiet. Out on Cape Cod Bay, the underpowered, outclassed Coast Guard was doing their best to combat the flood of illegal alcohol into Cape Codders' thirsty gullets.

If ever there was a land ideally suited for the landing of booze, it was Cape Cod. Its miles of shallow waters, creeks, rivers, and inlets directly off the deep ocean, coupled with a ready supply of some of the world's best small boat seaman, made the Cape a natural site for offloading clandestine cargo. Some took advantage of this opportunity.

Warren told of some prohibition happenings in Cape Cod Bay. He had a quahog dragger, a tired twenty-four-foot Crosby catboat. He worked the waters off Wellfleet's Jeremy's Point. At that time he lived in the Skaket area of Orleans and had a front row seat on the nights when the beleaguered Coast Guard and the bootleggers were embroiling themselves out on the bay waters. Experience had taught the watermen that when the midnight boat chases were taking place and the Coast Guard was getting too close for comfort, the bootleggers would take some hasty ranges as best they could in the darkness, then jettison the net-wrapped cases (twelve bottles per case) with the hopes of grappling for them at a quieter time.

This practice of jettisoning the cases was a time of opportunity for the local fishermen who fished that same bottom every working day. The roaring motors late at night was the signal for quahoggers to keep their eyes peeled the next day. They were looking for the telltale square shape of a case of alcohol (dubbed, box fish) on the bay bottom, easily seen in the shallow waters around Billingsgate Shoal.

An old Cape saying was: "On the first day of May, you can see the bottom of the Bay," which gives some idea of the clarity of those shoal waters, particularly in the springtime.

Why did these otherwise law-abiding men bring in this contraband? At least partly it was because they didn't see Prohibition as a serious law. They recognized that it was bound to be repealed fairly soon. Another factor was the profit in the trade. Warren, by working a ten- to twelve-hour day and manipulating a sixty-foot pole with a thirty-pound iron rake on the end, could clear five dollars a day. One bottle of booze would bring five dollars, a case, sixty dollars, and all the bay bottom boxes were cases.

Today, those amounts don't sound like much cash but back then, sixty dollars equaled more than two weeks of work. How many people today would walk away from two weeks' pay just lying there for the taking? Not many. They didn't back in the 1920s either.

One of the fishermen, Cal (Warren's brother), hoping to avoid detection, rigged an inconspicuous pipe up through the bottom of his craft. The line attaching the case to the boat was brought up through this pipe and the case was carried snugged to the boat's bottom, invisible to all. In the unhappy and unlikely event the officials were at the dock when Cal came in, he could cut the case loose for a later pickup and none the wiser. The only time he had to use this ingenious scheme, all didn't go just as planned.

The contraband case was retrieved from the bay bottom and firmly secured in the cleverly designed underwater holding device. As he approached the Rock Harbor docks, he saw trouble ahead on the caplog—the glint of a badge, the peaked hat, trouble in a blue uniform.

Undaunted, he inconspicuously reached down and unfastened the restraining line. Now there was nothing to connect him with any contraband. He was home free. The scheme worked for as long as it took the boat to travel eight feet, at which point the flaw in the plan made itself evident. The stoutly built, coarse net-covered wooden case was larger than the depth of water under the boat. Right in the harbor entrance, right under the nose of the uniformed official, there was a horrendous grinding and the tinkle of smashed glass, as the fishing boat rolled and lurched its way over the disintegrating case to dockside.

"Well Cal, what do ya suppose ya hit? Never knew there was anything in the harbor to bounce you around like that," the deputy said.

Cal knew the deputy, a fellow townsman, who probably had a pretty good idea what the obstruction was.

" Probably one of those sixty dollar rocks." Cal said.

The real indignity showed up the next morning when Cal fired up the old Ford engine to head out to the quahog beds for another try at whatever presented itself. As he engaged the clutch, the old boat instantly developed palsy, a violent shaking. The trip over the hooch had bent the shaft. It was a costly business getting the shaft straightened and replacing the shaft bearing—but other than that, the idea was foolproof. It was quite a while before Cal was able to forget about his road to easy riches. On the rare occasions when the memory of his fiasco was dimming, his fishermen friends were quick to remind him of that sixty dollar rock experienced that one time in the entrance to Rock Harbor.

Every fisherman has exciting times now and again. My old friend Warren told of his brush with defying gravity.

Warren's stout, old, twenty-four-foot catboat was one he had bought from a Chatham man, a Mr. Chase of Chase and Sandborn coffee. She was powered with a converted Ford Model A engine. The mast had long since been removed.

Like Cal, his brother, like most of us, Warren was always scheming to better himself, trying to find ways to do things faster and easier. With a system of lines and pulleys he rigged a primitive flying bridge so he could steer from the cabin top rather than down in the cockpit. The increased height gave him a vastly improved vantage point to spot those "box fish" that all the fisherman were looking for. And in twelve feet of water off Billingsgate Island, spot one he did. Warren was ready. He cast over the marker buoy with its anchor and maneuvered the big catboat until it was securely anchored right over that sixty dollar case. Then it was just a matter of bringing it aboard. He tried the grapnel. Nothing. The usual coarse burlap covering was not over the case. It couldn't be grapneled. He tried hooking it with a sharpened drail (a good-sized bass hook) to no avail. And there it was, twelve feet away, two weeks pay only twelve feet away—he could practically reach it.

Warren wasn't about to leave. Somehow, by some means, that case was going home with him. He couldn't leave two weeks pay just lying there. The thought occurred that if he could get down to that case, there was a good chance he could sink the sharp grapnel hooks into the side of the wooden case, come back aboard, and haul it up. He saw as no detriment to the plan that he, like most fishermen, couldn't swim a stroke.

He stripped down to the buff, tied a rope around his middle so he could haul himself back to the boat, and readied the grapnel hook. Warren studied and studied the situation, figured just what he had to do, and when all was in readiness, he launched himself from the cabin top.

In his own words, he recounted the experience:

"I was ready, had the hook in my right hand, ready to make my first ever dive. I had my eyes shut when I pushed off, but for some reason I opened them just before I hit the water. There, right under me, was the biggest dammed shark I'd ever seen. That gray back looked as big as a landing field. I don't know how it happened, but the next thing I knew I was back on that deck. Dry."

The pursuit of that easy money led to some strange behavior out in the bay. Perhaps none stranger than that gravity-defying dive.

After getting his heartbeat back to normal, Warren considered some more. There would be no more aquatic excursions. Case retrieval would have to be done from the surface. The few more attempts with the grapnel were fruitless. Then inspiration struck. He lashed two oars together to make a rigid pole long enough to reach that hard-to-get case. He then lashed a newly sharpened gaff to one of the oars, fished around for a few minutes until he secured good purchase on the crate and hauled it to the surface.

He finished up the day quahogging and came in with a satisfied smile on his face. When Warren called his buyer friend, a man who had a standing order with most of the fishermen, that gentleman also had a satisfied smile on his face. That one-time, two-or-three-year migration of "box fish" into Cape Cod Bay was time for quiet, satisfied smiles all across Cape Cod. And some families are smiling yet.

But Warren didn't always wear a smile.

During the Second World War, pilot whales (cousins of the beautiful, sleek dolphins), the big animals that still strand each year near Wellfleet's Lieutenant's Island, were called upon to contribute to the war effort. During the war Warren was a deep water quahogger out in Cape Cod Bay. He told me that early in the war some military types appeared on the scene. They gathered the fishermen together and asked if they could get some blackfish oil. Apparently this oil, unlike all others, didn't congeal at the high altitudes the planes were flying; whale oil was the perfect oil for the complex, many-faceted bomb sights. The fishermen were pretty sure they could deliver the necessary oil, and they were right. When one of the fisherman sighted the dorsal fins of these air-breathing animals he immediately signaled the others to gather around the outside of the school to begin the drive. They would bang oars on the water, rev their engines and generally make an unholy commotion, driving the frightened animals into the shallow water on the ebbing tide. There they stranded and suffocated by their own weight. The fishermen would then set about the bloody and grisly task of extracting the oil of these easily driven, harmless animals. A sad thing.

But if it shortened the war, it saved human lives and that made it an acceptable tradeoff.

We have all done things that seemed fine when we did them but on reflection would never do again. Near the end of his life Warren told me that of all the things he had done in his life, one of the few things he wouldn't do again was drive blackfish. Their moans and sighs (as if in resigned reproach) as they died slowly on the drying flats was something that still reverberated in his mind.

But rise to a challenge? With Warren all one had to do was offer a challenge and he was ready. Warren had experienced about everything most Cape Codders ever do in a lifetime, but he was always ready for whatever came along. What came along was a suggestion from me that we bring a twenty-two-foot triple hulled boat down from Boston. It was a used boat I had purchased at a good price; all we needed was to get it to the Cape. Trailering it would have been the easy way but neither Warren or I had ever taken the trip by water. So we decided to sample the aquatic route. I had purchased the boat in February and by mid-March she was ready to go. I called my old friend and asked for his best weather prediction and I was asking for a lot.

Anyone who has spent any time on the Cape knows that March is a time of uneasy weather, and very little of that weather is good. Warren did his best and pronounced that the next three days would be relatively calm, good for the hundred-mile boat trip, and added that he was ready and raring to go.

We made the arrangements on the Boston end. The flight from Provincetown was flawless. We were met at Logan by the boat sellers. It was a short ride to the marina where the sleek and purring boat awaited us. Except for some instructions on how to signal the bridge to open it was all pretty routine. At this point Warren's predictions were right on. It was sunny with just a light southwest breeze—perfect weather for the trip along the South Shore. We were both excited and ready. So apparently was the boat. The little V-6 engine could barely be heard; it was just purring away, as though it too, was anxious to undertake this journey. The boat was like new; there was no sign of use or abuse that we could see on its exterior, or hear in that smoothly running engine.

Down the river to the first obstruction, a low bridge—a few toots with the air horn and like magic the bridge lifted and on we went. It was under the Tobin Bridge then, down by old Ironsides sitting so stolidly in her longtime berth and then out into historic Boston Harbor. The harbor islands looked quite resplendent in their greening early spring garb. Their isolation and quiet were in direct counterpoint to the hubbub of the teeming city so close by. Out of the harbor we turned south down past Minot's Ledge Light, a lighthouse on a rocky outcropping, seemingly far at sea. Then Duxbury was passing by and beautiful and inviting Plymouth, where it all began more than three hundred years ago with the arrival of the Pilgrims.

The Cape Cod Canal, too, had an inviting look, and this was an invitation we readily accepted. It was the first time either of us had been under the canal bridges; they looked so much more impressive from the water than our usual car bound view. But as we turned the corner by the Maritime Academy, the weather began to unravel. Warren's reputation as a weather forecaster, which had until now approached impeccable status, suffered somewhat. What had been a calm sea now became lumpy and topped with white froth. What had been a sunny day with light to variable winds changed dramatically as we sped out of the canal. The sunny day deteriorated into gray murk, the light winds went somewhere for reinforcements and returned with what Warren labeled a "white-assed sou'wester." This was a term I'd never heard before but apt, this expression was apt.

It was rough and our little chip of a boat didn't like the conditions at all. Buzzard's Bay has a deserved reputation for turbulent water and it lived up to its billing. That strong southwest wind blowing directly into the narrowing confines of that rock bordered bay made massive, steep, froth-topped waves the norm. Up and over these billows of water we went, with sluices of icy spray flying across and into the cockpit. About every fifteen minutes or so, on a particularly steep comber, the propeller would come clear of the water with an accompanying, screaming complaint from the engine. Rough? Yes, it was rough all right.

Salt water stings the eyes and the continual icy showers we were enduring did little to improve our vision. What we were looking for was the narrow, all but invisible channel through the Elizabeth Islands that would bring us out into Nantucket Sound by Woods Hole.

I don't think we ever would have discovered the well-hidden

entrance except that the only boat we saw that day happened along. It was the Coast Guard out searching for a lost boat. They overlooked the fact that we had no registration, no numbers, and no life jackets; instead they pointed us in the right direction and wished us well.

When we finally turned the corner into Woods Hole Pass, the turbulence ceased and blessed calm prevailed. I asked Warren if he wanted me to call for someone to come get him. He was stung to the quick. Rarely have I seen him so outraged.

" Ride home, ride home? Hell no. If the boat can stand it, if you can stand it, so can I," he said. He knew the trip across Nantucket Sound would be much easier than the previous hour's slog through the billowing head seas and how right he was.

We were going with the waves now and that bluff bow rode over those watery hills with aplomb and scarcely a jolt. By comparison it was a luxurious ride. At one point we slid by the Shenandoah, a sizeable sailing ship, with all her sails set. It was a stirring sight, a sight that might have been commonplace a hundred years ago but now was quite spectacular for its uniqueness and the soaring beauty of those taut white sails. While watching this magnificent ship I was also looking at Warren. He, too, was unique. I wondered how many seventy-five-year-olds would look as sprightly after being pounded so violently for an hour or more, all the while being drenched with March seawater that was still dripping from every part of his anatomy. I suspected not many.

We soon slipped past the big white sailing ship and continued east across the sound. The trip home was anti-climatic, smooth, fast, and enjoyable. My old friend's weather-predicting reputation was everafter less than sterling, but his reputation as a shipmate had gained sterling luster.

* * *

"Save the best till last" seems to characterize Cape Cod in the fall. Fall is the prettiest season of the Cape's year—a time of lingering summer. The water that surrounds this peninsula stays warm long into the fall, a gentle transition to winter's rigors. Many of these fall days are cloudless, windless, blue-skyed, and just the right temperature—perfect flying days. If nature offers such treats it would seem a shame not to take advantage of them. I called Warren. "It's a great day for flying. How about going over to Tuckernuck? There's something there I'd like to show you."

Tuckernuck is a small island off the west end of Nantucket, part of the glacial moraine that is Nantucket. It was once connected to the main island, but erosion has whittled away the connecting link. It's now a lovely separate island. The few buildings found there are for the most part substantial structures, old gracious homes. And there was one in particular I wanted to show Warren. I'd landed there before. Two dirt roads intersected on the grassy plains on the island's south side. No matter the wind direction—upwind landings were a cinch as long as the plane stayed in the well-worn ruts.

Warren, by this time was seventy-eight and semi-retired. He didn't have anything pressing on his slate. He'd really enjoy the trip. Warren was a game friend, game for anything that sounded interesting and almost everything sounded interesting. The proposed trip was right up his alley. He loved to fly, and this trip would enable him to visit a piece of the region he had never been on and he would be able to do it all in comfort.

His angina precluded any long-distance walking in the cold weather. I promised only short walks, as I thought it possible to taxi to the site I wanted to show him. The dirt roads we were to land on wandered all over the island, connecting the houses in a loose web of ruts.

We agreed on a time, met at Chatham Airport, rented the little two-seat silvery Cessna-150, and in the tight confines of the cockpit, left Chatham's runway on a southwesterly heading, bound for Tuckernuck by way of one of Cape Cod's jewels, Monomoy. Nature's beauty surrounds us here on the Cape; Monomoy from the air epitomizes the Cape's beauty.

From the wild cranberry bogs, the large freshwater ponds, the miles of white sand beaches, the crashing surf, the acres of sandbars and clam flats, to the soaring dunes, this island is the inspiration for artists and a source of solace for us ordinary mortals. Warren had never seen Monomoy from the air, though he had been on the island many times. This high vantage point, about 1200 feet, gave a seldom-seen perspective to my old friend.

"God, it's beautiful. Look at those ducks on that little pond. Geese too. God." He was all excited, and despite his long association with his land, his excitement had a grounding in reverence. As so often happens in the company of passionate people, his enthusiasm and reverence communicated itself to me. Through his eyes, I also was seeing this land for the first time. Things I had seen many times before took on a new aura. Soon, I too was excitedly pointing out the sights of this picturesque ten-mile finger of white sand. The little Cessna droned over Monomoy in about ten minutes as we climbed to 6,000 feet for the eleven-mile overwater stretch to Nantucket's Great Point. We followed, the north shore of the big island around to Madaket to the accompaniment of Warren's enthusiastic commentary about the schools of bluefish and the occasional big bass clearly seen in the shallow waters fringing the island, and by the way, just how big were those fish?

Tuckernuck was a very short hop. We circled the island, lined up on the appropriate road, and bounced in to a rough landing. The little Cessna had a tricycle landing gear, a type of gear that gives the pilot great visibility as a tradeoff for the propeller being quite close to the ground.

On normal runways the ground clearance of the propeller is of little consequence. Unless the pilot does something very wrong it will never hit.

As we got out of the plane and felt the chill of the air and the brisk breeze, Warren reminded me again of his angina. When he saw how far we had to walk he decided against making such a strenuous effort.

"That's no problem, no problem at all," I said. "Hop back in the plane, crank up the heater. We'll taxi over to the house."

I'd checked out which of the dirt roads I thought led to the particular house I wanted to show him. This road had been little used. The grass was about knee high between the ruts and the propeller acted as a vertical lawnmower as we jounced slowly along. Grass, sticks, and twigs were flying by the side windows as we cut a swath en route to the large house. The road deteriorated as we approached, deteriorated to the point that we couldn't find it at all. We were headed in the right direction but were now going cross-country, or cross-field. It didn't seem to make much difference; the ride was still bouncy and the volume of debris flying by the windows increased somewhat, but otherwise there was no problem.

Just as I was about to stop, one of the wheels found a nice little woodchuck hole. When the wheel dropped about ten inches so did the propeller, which dropped about two inches below ground level. The maelstrom of grass and twigs was joined by much harder stuff—sand and small rocks that started ricocheting off the fuselage, beating a brisk tatoo on the thin aluminum skin. What a racket. I shut her off and we got out to inspect the damage. I had visions of being stranded on this remote island. No one knew where we were, and I knew the flying service that had rented us the plane would take a dim view of their chariot in such a spot. Indeed, I vaguely remembered that we weren't supposed to land on any dirt strips with these planes, let alone go taxiing cross-country. But that little Cessna had a toughness. Aside from a few nicks, paint scrapings, and newly burnished propeller tips, there was no apparent damage despite the cacophony in the cockpit.

We were now close enough to make an easy stroll to the nearest house and what I had wanted to show Warren. As we approached, the most visible feature on the lawn was a try pot, one of those enormous black iron kettles used on shipboard to try out whale blubber.

Nantucket's whaling heritage is ever-present, this huge iron try pot a reminder of those long-ago times. As we crossed the lawn to the old black pot, the scenario that I wanted my friend to see was displayed before us—a complete whale skeleton arrayed as if the defunct whale had been fed into the pot a piece at a time and the remains arranged in proper whale shape on the lawn. This was a singular lawn decoration, a whale-sized lawn ornament. Warren, with a lifetime on the water was intrigued as I knew he would be. He waxed enthusiastically about that magnificent pot and its probable origins. Where had it been and how had it landed on this remote lawn? The other big mystery was the skeleton. We paced it off—fifty-five feet from nose to tail. It represented several tons of whale flesh.

Again, how had it arrived here as a lawn ornament?

We made some conjectures, but couldn't really comprehend how it happened to land on the lawn of the old house. It was, and is, a whale-sized mystery. We had assumed we were alone on the little island but such was not the case. A slow-moving, heavily bundled figure emerged from one of the nearby houses. Whoever it was, with halting steps and two canes, was headed our way. We walked down to meet this person, an elderly lady, who turned out to be one of the Nantucket Coffins, among the oldest names on the island.

At one point Warren and Mrs. Coffin were deeply engrossed in conversation. I was looking at the two of them both sharing respected old Cape names, to the marsh beyond, across the water to the western tip of Nantucket, thinking of all the Cape history these two had seen and influenced in their lifetimes. I knew Warren was by nature an optimist, so too, obviously, was this rugged old lady. They were a pleasure to be around, good role models.

She let us know she was all alone here on Tuckernuck, that she liked it that way because the big island was too crowded for her taste. She had this old family home on the small island and it was just what she wanted. At 83, she was damn-well going to do just what she wanted to do. Her grandson came over from Madaket to check on her every couple of days to bring her food, help bring in the wood, and care for the place. She told us if she really needed anything quickly, she only had to lower the flag. Her son, a pilot for a local airline, flew right over her house twice a day. A down flag meant she needed help. Here was a lady with grit. She could barely walk, she was quite overweight, yet she was going it alone with a wood stove for heat and a hand pump for water.

Warren and I spent at least half an hour talking with her. Had it not been so cold we would have stayed longer. Her stories were fascinating; the fact of her staying on this little bit of paradise all by herself was the fodder for great stories.

We finally said our goodbys and trekked back to the plane. I pried the wheels up out of the woodchuck hole and yanked and tugged the craft around to head us back. The wings were still attached, the tail was where it belonged, everything checked out. It was just a matter of turning the key, taxiing back to the road, taking off, and heading home.

That was our script, but that little Cessna had a slightly different version, one that included further testing of our fortitude. Turning the key normally started the engine. On this occasion turning the key produced a clunk. There were more turns, more clunks, and no engine starting.

What now? Here we were on a remote island where I knew we really weren't supposed to be, in a plane whose only language was "clunk."

"Can you start this thing by spinning the prop?" Warren queried.

" I guess so, I've never done it," I answered. "I've seen it done though. I'll give it a whirl."

We thought it through. I told Warren to hold his feet tight on the brakes. It's a little frightening to stand inches from an aluminum blade that could easily kill you and then try to coax it to life. I pulled it through a couple of times and the blessed thing roared to life. What a sweet sound and a fine feeling that was. All the way back to Chatham, Warren was worrying about Mrs. Coffin, wondering if he should call the authorities to have her checked more often, worrying about her health.

But mostly we both admired her steadfast determination to stick it out in the place she so obviously loved with no electricity and no running water. I think we both wondered if, given the same circumstances, we would have done the same thing. I'd like to think I would have, and I expect Warren would have too..

We both admired her courage. But Warren, too, had displayed the same kind of courage many times in his life. He had also displayed the same love of the land of his birth.

That very next fall Warren and I were out in back of Sampson's Island looking for a duck or two. It was a miserable day, a windy, freezing rain kind of a day, a near-perfect duck day. But the birds weren't flying and we were slowly congealing as the icy rain soaked up our sleeves and ran down our necks.

This gruff guy—this seventy-eight-year-old native Cape Codder—had done all kinds of things to provide a living for his family. He'd been a cranberry grower, a commercial shellfisherman, a commercial finfisherman, a minor league real estate buyer and seller, and I'm sure he was involved in many other enterprises. He was an enterprising man whose endeavors never failed for the lack of hard work or quick intelligence. This man who had seen and done it all, looked at me, icicles forming on his hat brim, all but numb with the cold and rain, and summed up a lifetime of living on his beloved Cape Cod.

"God boy, ain't we lucky living on Cape Cod? Just ain't we lucky?"